HOW TO MAKE SUCCESSFUL SMALL CLAIMS

A guide to court procedure and alternative dispute resolution

By Anthony Reeves

HOW TO MAKE SUCCESSFUL SMALL CLAIMS

By Anthony Reeves

Copyright Notice:

© Anthony Reeves 2014

ISBN: 978-1-291-89073-0

Acknowledgments

I would like to thank FAB.

In memory of Buster.

Crown copyright material is reproduced with the permission of the Controller of HMSO and the Queen's Printer of Scotland (licence number: C02W0002748)

CONTENTS:

Chapter:

PREFACE

There are many claims that are issued in the County Court[1], but only around 4% end up going to a hearing. Out of the cases that go to a hearing, the vast majority are small claims. In the first quarter of 2013, there were 10,682 trials - 7,410 of those being small claims hearings. With the small claims limit having increased in April 2013 to £10,000, this will have an impact on the number of cases in the small claims track. The statistics show that small claims make up the vast majority of claims that are in the County Court and probably explain some of the recent measures by the Ministry of Justice to persuade litigants to use alternative methods to resolve a dispute, such as the Court's small claims telephone mediation service.

A defended claim that does not exceed £10,000 will normally be conducted in the small claims procedure of the County Court. This level for small claims was recently increased from £5,000. To many people and small businesses, a claim for just under £10,000 would not be regarded as small, but in legal terms such claims are a given a more simplified and streamlined procedure. The fact that legal costs are not normally awarded in small claims means that it is more likely that the case will not be conducted by lawyers and the vast majority of the cases will conducted by a litigants in person. Add to this the fact that court fees have risen quite steeply making small claims expensive to bring, it is even more important that you know what you are doing and how to increase your chances of winning. The aim of this book is not simply focused on the legal processes of making a small claim. An important part of the book addresses the growing requirements for alternative dispute resolution ("ADR"). As will be seen later, there are situations where the parties to a dispute are well advised to use ADR.

Many people - lawyers included - may think that a case will be decided by a District Judge consistently applying the law to cases before him or her. That would be great if that was the reality. The fact is that court action is becoming much more unpredictable. Gone are the days when a lawyer will say to a client, "I think your case has *X% prospect of success*". In

---

[1] Court Statistics Quarterly January to March 2013, published 20 June 2013 stated that in 2011, 1,504,243 claims were issued.

recent years, I have been involved in many cases where the outcome has been unexpected. Although legal expenses insurers like to get opinions as to the percentage chances of winning before offering cover, many lawyers will couch their opinions in a non committal way which emphasizes the uncertainty in the process. With the reality being that a party is not likely to bother with an appeal for reasons of costs if for no other, the rather arbitrary nature of a small claims hearing is what you are faced with and so making the best of that brief opportunity to put your case across to a busy and time constrained Judge is what it is all about.

Before you even consider embarking on a court claim, you should make a realistic assessment of whether your efforts are actually going to get you your money from the Defendant. It is a very old cliché - but still true - that you *"can't get blood from a stone"*. This should always be your first consideration. If you have any serious doubts about getting your money after winning your case, then don't put yourself through the stress and expense of making a court claim. If there is some doubt about the financial status of your opponent and a reasonable offer is made to settle the case it would be very sensible to accept it because - in the long run - it might be that your overall return does not beat this offer. Considering alternative means of settling the dispute, such as arbitration provided by a professional body or mediation, is also a sensible idea. Obviously the costs and how genuine the other side is in wanting to reach a settlement are important factors in deciding whether to go for mediation because you don't want to spend further costs and waste more time if the Defendant is simply using it to gain more time to avoid making payment. There is also the danger that, with the increase in court fees, many Defendants will simply wait to see if you can afford to start a claim before considering making a payment. With court fees expected to increase and the likelihood of the small claims limit being raised to £15,000 in the not too distance future, this may result in paying for some form of ADR becoming an even more attractive and cost effective strategy.

In addition to the change in the financial limit for small claims there is the another significant change in that you can no longer pop down to your local County Court to issue your claim (if the claim is for a monetary consideration). There are two ways of issuing a money claim; it can either be done using "Money Claim Online" or on paper by sending the completed Claim Form to the County Court Money Claims Centre in Salford. This new administrative centre opened during March 2012 and it deals with the early stages of a money claim. If the case becomes defended then it is sent out to the appropriate court for a hearing. With effect from April 2014, there is only one unified "County Court" and all the local County Courts are merely to be referred to as "hearing centres".

Obtaining a County Court Judgment is often easier than realising the money you have been awarded by the court. There are various procedures for enforcing a Judgment (collecting your money if the Defendant has not paid) but it is reasonable to expect that these methods can potentially be slow and ineffective. This is probably due to a combination of procedures that lack the desired weight and substance - for example; bailiffs not having powers of uninvited/forced entry or data protection laws that make it difficult to obtain financial information about individuals. In April 2014 the government implemented reforms to bailiff law and these changes will make it more difficult for High Court Enforcement Agents to recover debts. One of the provisions that have an impact on the success of enforcement officers is the new rule requiring seven days notice to be given to the Judgment debtor before the enforcement agent can attend to make an attempt to take control of the debtor's goods. Therefore, before starting a small claim, it is vital to consider how you would get your money once you have a court Judgment.

Although District Judges are helpful to litigants in person, they certainly prefer those, who venture into their courtrooms, to have taken reasonable steps to prepare their case properly so that that the nature of the claim is clear and there is supporting evidence in the form of documents or witness statements. Having read this book thoroughly you should have a sound understanding of how to prepare a small claim. Just because a claim is within the small claims track does not mean that it is acceptable for sloppy presentation; a proportionate and limited amount of time will be allocated to a small claim, so it is imperative that the nature of the case is instantly clear as soon as the District Judge picks up the papers. Although this book is primarily designed for litigants in person, trainee lawyers, seeking a starting point for putting together a small claim, may also find this book useful.

May 2014

Chapter 1

Alternatives to Court and Pre-Action Letters

There was a time when all that a Claimant needed to do - before issuing a court claim - was to send a brief letter before action, informing the Defendant that, unless payment was received within 7 days, court action would be commenced. In the *current* climate a court would regard this as insufficient; proper exchange of information and attempts to settle amicably are expected before *any* papers are sent to court. This "pre-action" conduct is seen as a major, and necessary, aspect of litigation[2].

Although called "pre-action" conduct, there should be no expectation or presumption that the matter will culminate in court action. Indeed, the commencement of court action should be the *last* resort and the courts do not expect the parties to go through the motions, otherwise associated with pre-action conduct, during the stages leading up to a hearing; real and demonstrable attempts to settle, prior to the issue of proceedings, are expected. Otherwise, any unreasonable behaviour may be penalised by cost sanctions. If there is a prospect of the matter being resolved, without the need for formal legal action, then the possibility should be explored. The skill is being able to identify when a dispute will benefit from alternative dispute resolution. Expertise in the field will help identify the types of cases. A party in a dispute will often believe that their case is watertight; therefore, why should they compromise? They feel that attaining everything to satisfy their argument is the only point at which they will be prepared to stop; anything less and they "will see the other party in court". Such fighting talk is understandable; however, a party can become overly obsessed with the dispute and, consequently, they risk failing to address - or reflect on - the issues objectively. This is even true of lawyers; they can potentially turn out to be terrible clients. What this means is that, even though lawyers may possess knowledge of applicable law, they may not be able to step back and objectively weigh up whether or not there is a better way of resolving the dispute other than launching into court action.

The layperson is not expected to know all of the relevant pre-action

---

[2] Litigation is the term used by lawyers to describe the act or process of bringing legal action.

procedure(s) or, indeed, the court rules throughout the life of a small claim, but the rules are readily available online at the Court Service website and so anyone can look at what is expected; at least in general terms. The rules that govern claims in the County Court of England & Wales are known as the Civil Procedure Rules (commonly referred to as "CPR"). The CPR contains 82 Parts and, in addition, a "Practice Direction" supplements each Part. Practice Directions contain guidance on how to interpret the rules as well as setting out further requirements of civil court procedure. There are also a number of "Pre-Action Protocols" which set out the steps to be followed in particular types of cases. CPR guidance can be found on the Court Service website at:

http://www.justice.gov.uk/courts/procedure-rules/civil/rules

It would be useful to be familiar with some Parts of the CPR and the pre-action protocols before making a small claim. The important ones are:

- Practice Direction - Pre-action Conduct:
The steps the parties are expected to follow before starting a court claim.

- CPR Part 1: "The Overriding Objective"
The overall purpose of the court rules which is to deal with cases justly and at proportionate cost.

- CPR Part 7: "How to Start Proceedings - The Claim Form"
These are the rules that govern the issuing of proceedings. It would also be useful to read some of the relevant parts of the accompanying Practice Direction.

- CPR Part 27: "The Small Claims Track"
This Part contains the special procedure that applies to cases that are allocated to the small claims track.

Pre-action protocol

The aims of pre-action protocol are;

> *"(1) enable parties to settle the issue between them without the need to start proceedings (a court claim); and*
> *(2) support the efficient management by the court and the parties of proceedings that cannot be avoided."*

These aims are to be achieved by encouraging the parties to –

(1) exchange information about the issue, and
(2) consider using a form of Alternative Dispute Resolution ('ADR').

The use of alternative forms of dispute resolution (ADR) is a very important ingredient of pre-action conduct. As will be seen later, the pre-action protocol letter should, where appropriate, suggest an alternative means of resolving the dispute.

There are various pre-action protocols, including:

Protocol	Date
Personal Injury	26 April 1999
Clinical Disputes	26 April 1999
Construction and Engineering	2 October 2000
Defamation	2 October 2000
Professional Negligence	16 July 2001
Judicial Review	4 March 2002
Disease and Illness	8 December 2003
Housing Disrepair	8 December 2003
Possession Claims based on rent arrears	2 October 2006
Possession Claims based on Mortgage Arrears etc.	19 November 2008
Dilapidations (commercial property)	1 January 2012

The type of claim that a litigant in person, or a small business, is most likely to make - through the small claims procedure - include debt claims and consumer matters; this type of claim typically arises out of a breach of contract. For a claim of this nature, where there is no *specific* protocol, there are two general protocols contained in "Annex A" and "Annex B" to the Practice Direction on pre-action conduct. It is these two protocols that will mostly affect claims that proceed in the small claims procedure and so it is these which this chapter will concentrate on:

Annex A
This Annex sets out detailed guidance on a pre-action procedure that is likely to satisfy the court in most circumstances where no pre-action protocol or other formal pre-action procedure applies. It is intended as a guide for parties, particularly those without legal representation, in straightforward claims that are likely to be disputed. It is not intended to apply to debt claims where it is not disputed that the money is owed and where the Claimant follows a statutory or other formal pre-action procedure."

Annex B

Information to be provided in a debt claim where the Claimant is a business and the Defendant is an individual:

(1) Provide details of how the money can be paid (for example the method of payment and the address to which it can be sent);
(2) State that the Defendant can contact the Claimant to discuss possible repayment options, and provide the relevant contact details; and
(3) Inform the Defendant that free independent advice and assistance can be obtained from organisations including those listed in the table below.

INDEPENDENT ADVICE ORGANISATIONS

Organisation	Address	Telephone Number	e-mail Address
National Debtline	Tricorn House 51-53 Hagley Road Edgbaston Birmingham B16 8TP	FREEPHONE 0808 808 4000	www.nationaldebtline.co.uk
Consumer Credit Counselling Service (CCCS)		FREEPHONE 0800 138 1111	www.cccs.co.uk
Citizens Advice	Check your local Yellow Pages or Thomson local directory for address and telephone numbers		www.citizensadvice.org.uk
Community Legal Advice (formerly Community		0845 345 4345	www.clsdirect.org.uk

Alternatives to Court Action

It is wise to pause and consider - if you have not already done so - the alternatives to starting a County Court action. The County Court rules require parties involved in a dispute to consider alternatives to court action. In some situations, if a party unreasonably refuses to consider Alternative Dispute Resolution (ADR) then a court has the power to penalize that party by an award of costs.

There is undoubtedly a link between the pressure to use ADR and the unwillingness of successive governments to spend further resources on the civil courts. However, putting aside the motives for the push to more ADR, it has to be acknowledged that there are situations that certainly benefit from using other ways of settling a dispute. The skill is being able to recognise a case that would benefit from ADR and make use of it at the appropriate time. In recent times, the courts have taken the view that all cases can benefit from ADR. What *I* believe this means is that if you view "ADR" as any form of communication between the parties then that could be of benefit as it may narrow the issues or reveal that there is no merit in the claim.

There are various methods of alternative dispute resolution including:

- Mediation
- Arbitration
- Adjudication
- Expert determination
- Early Neutral Evaluation

Essentially, all the various methods of ADR are trying to get the parties to discuss or at least focus on the relevant issues so that a resolution might be achieved. Some of the above, such as Adjudication and Expert Determination resolve the dispute, i.e. the process itself decides who wins, whereas other forms of ADR, such as mediation, attempt to get the parties to come to an acceptable agreement. If a deal is done, it should be recorded in a way that becomes legally enforceable if either party goes back on the deal. If either party breaches the agreement then it would be a simple case of issuing a claim for a breach of contract.

Being able to recognise whether a case could be resolved by ADR is not necessarily something a layperson could be expected to know and so seeking legal advice at an early stage, as to the merits of your case, is vital. If your claim revolves around mainly oral evidence, with little in the way of supporting documentation, to evidence your case, you should be prepared to mitigate your claim. This can be a difficult view to adopt, as it is easy to feel strongly that your case is entirely sound and consequently push for total victory. The challenge is being able to predict the outcome of a small claim based predominantly on oral evidence from witnesses whose memories will naturally fade over time; it is sometimes not much better than simply tossing a coin. This, to a certain degree, explains why lawyers do not give clear-cut evaluations of the prospects of success; there may seem a tendency to sit on the fence. Whilst there is the obvious worry of a complaint, if it goes horribly wrong, it is usually as a result of solid experience gained by the lawyer in the courtroom. I have been involved with cases where the anticipated result leaned heavily in favour of one party, only to turn up at court and discover that either your case finds *no* favour with the District Judge or, for whatever reason, the case does not come across in the best light. District Judges usually do not see case papers very long before a hearing and are expected to grasp the key pieces of evidence immediately. The reality is that small claims hearings are squeezed into a busy County Court list and the time constraint means that the case does not always receive as much attention as the lay person may expect - or think it deserves. This is not a criticism of District Judges, but a statement of the fact that County Courts are under severe pressure and do not always have the resources to cope with demand.

So, returning to the key question of whether a case might benefit from some alternative dispute resolution procedure and what type of ADR might be appropriate, let us consider some different types of disputes (by way of brief case study) to explore the best ways of resolving the issues:

John Bird Communications v. New Marketing Ltd

John Bird is a PR executive who recently set up in business on his own. Among the services he provides, is artwork and the production of magazines. New Marketing Ltd has recently acquired a contract to provide newsletters. John Bird meets with Frances Taylor at New Marketing Ltd and they come to an arrangement whereby in return for a monthly retainer of £1,750, John Bird will provide his services to assist in the production of the newsletters. It was further agreed that this arrangement would continue for the duration of New Marketing's contract to produce the newsletters. Nothing was put in writing to evidence the terms of the agreement. However, New Marketing Ltd paid the retainer for nine months. In February, Frances Taylor contacts John Bird by telephone and says that she no longer requires his services with immediate effect. John reminds Frances that there are 2 months remaining of the

> *contract left to produce newsletters and so he should be paid for the rest of that period, especially as he has prepared material for these two months and had also turned down other work so that he could complete the tasks for New Marketing Ltd. John Bird writes to Frances and claims the 2 months of the remaining retainer he claims he is due, namely £3,500. Frances replies by saying there was no contractual term stipulating that their business arrangement would be for the duration of the newsletter contract and disputes that he is owed anything.*

This is a classic example of a dispute arising where there is no documentary evidence to support the main premise of the argument. It is a classic trap that business people fall into because they trust the other person they are working with and never see the need to formalize the main terms of their working arrangement on paper. This type of case could, of course, proceed to a small claims hearing, with each party turning up to a court and giving oral evidence as to what they recall was the basis of the business arrangement. The uncertainty of the outcome is obvious. Before arriving at a court hearing, John Bird is going to spend approximately £500 on court fees plus the time in preparing the matter with the prospects being 50:50 at the very best. It is a very good example where mediation could be appropriate. It would be sensible for John to compromise the claim and if he could obtain, say £1,500, then it would be a good result. Some may view any mitigation as letting the debtor "get away with it", but there is a strong prospect of Mr Bird leaving the courtroom empty handed and several hundred pounds lighter in the pocket because of the court fees paid out.

In other situations, different types of ADR may be appropriate. If the facts are not in dispute (but there is a specific technical issue that needs deciding) the instructing of an expert to determine that issue would be a sensible way of resolving the matter. The following case is an example of where this form of dispute resolution might be appropriate:

Big Lorry Distributors and Round the Clock Maintenance

> *Big Lorry Distributors ("BLD") are a nationwide company that delivers a variety of products for businesses. They have a large fleet of lorries. They have all of their lorries serviced and repaired by Round the Clock Maintenance ("RCM"). BLD brought in one of its delivery lorries for a problem to be diagnosed and repaired by RCM. The lorry had been loosing power and there was an issue when*

changing gear. RCM diagnosed the fault as a requiring a new gearbox and a new one was fitted. The lorry was back out on the road but after only travelling a further 2,000 miles, the lorry began to lose power again. BLD took the vehicle back to RCM who said that the problem was not related to the previous repair and quoted BLD for further major repair in the region of £2,000. With the lorry off the road for a further week, BLD would also incur the costs of hiring a replacement lorry. BLD were not convinced that the problem was unrelated, and as the loss of power on the second occasion had very similar symptoms to the first breakdown, BLD suggested to RCM that the first repair had not be carried out correctly; this was something which was denied by RCM.

This is a classic case of two businesses that have had a good commercial relationship for a long period of time but have a dispute which could jeopardise their future dealings if not handled correctly. It seems imperative to take a realistic view of the situation; it is a dispute about a few thousand pounds and alternatives to simply suing for the money should be sought. In such a case, the parties should consider agreeing to instruct an independent engineer to examine the vehicle and give an expert opinion as to the cause of the new problem and whether it was due to any failure to exercise reasonable care and skill by RMC. If both parties agree in advance to be bound by the expert's opinion, it would be a sensible way of resolving the dispute and maintaining the commercial relationship.

When considering alternative methods of resolving a small claim, costs can be a key factor; especially in light of the general "no costs" rule in small claims cases. The cost of instructing an independent expert may not, in every case, be proportionate. However, the use of a method that decides the issues, such as adjudication or arbitration, may be cost justified because another form of ADR (such as mediation) does not automatically result in a decision but, instead, only seeks to attain agreement between the parties.

The obvious problem in small claims cases is that if you use an outside mediator who charges for their fees then it is unlikely that these costs will be recovered. There are companies in existence which are offering telephone or online mediation[3] at very reasonable prices for a typical duration of 2 to 3 hours. Spending a few hundred pounds for mediation, where you don't have to travel or fix up a venue with a couple of meeting

---

[3] www.small-claims-mediation.co.uk

rooms, has obvious attractions. The preparation for a mediation hearing usually involves providing the mediator with a position statement. However, in small claims mediation the position statement may not be as detailed as those mediations involving larger sums of money. Often, the telephone mediations provided by the Court Service will not involve sending a position statement beforehand; instead, the mediator will discuss your position on the telephone at the start of the process.

Even if the costs of small claims mediation is free, as is currently the case with the telephone mediation service provided by the courts, it could still, in some cases, add further costs to the parties involved. Cases have been reported, in legal journals, of cases that highlight this point. The types of cases tend to be where District Judges believe that a case is suitable for mediation but one of the parties challenge this but are warned by the Judge that, if they refuse mediation, they risk a costs order. So the parties go off and mediate and this incurs more time and, where the party has a lawyer advising, more costs. If the party, that was reluctant to mediate, is insistent on not conceding anything then the process achieves very little. Now, the obvious question is, "do you need a lawyer to be involved in a small claims telephone mediation?" There has also been frustration during these situations because – sometimes - the dispute involves, for example; an interpretation of a contract which, with hindsight, would have been better handled by a Judge (or some form of adjudicator).

Where the parties are opposed to mediation I have sometimes seen skilful Judges seize the moment and conduct the hearing in a manner akin to "neutral evaluation". It sometimes comes about by saying to the parties that they should take time to consider doing a deal outside the courtroom. He or she then sends them out to discuss the issues. They come back in and, in the event they have not reached an agreement, the District Judge may say, "I now don't have time to hear this case," and go on to give, if both parties agree, an overview of the strengths and weaknesses of both sides in the knowledge that it will be listed again on the first available date to be heard by a *different* Judge. These pronouncements usually make the parties take stock and recognise that perhaps winning is not going to be so straightforward as they had previously thought. If parties are prepared to compromise after getting a few home truths from the District Judge then it lends support to the fact that the parties are more likely to settle through an ADR process that gains the respect of the parties. This may be because of the standing of the person entrusted to try and settle the dispute. Early Neutral Evaluation is - in a way - rather like the District Judge telling the party a few "home truths" about the case, except it is explored at the *start* of the process. With the opinions of the evaluation ringing in their ears, they go away and find it easier to reach an agreement. Early Neutral Evaluation is a popular form of ADR in large commercial disputes, where perhaps a retired Judge or senior barrister is asked to give a neutral assessment, but, in small claims, this becomes cost prohibitive.

The reluctance to use some forms of ADR, such as mediation, is that a party may fear the other party is using the process as a way of a "fishing expedition" in order to discover information about the other side's case, and potentially discovering previously unknown weaknesses, without any genuine desire to settle.

The important point is not so much that the parties must use some third party to resolve their dispute, but they should at least be prepared to negotiate.

Pre-Action Letters

Sample Pre-action Protocol Letter – Commercial Debtor:

The following is a sample "letter before action" where the debtor is a business. The important aspect of the sample letter is that it sets out a clear summary of the facts and it refers to - and encloses - key documents. The information in the letter is sufficient for Blogs Engineering to respond fully to the claim. The letter suggests that Excellent Recruitment is prepared to consider ADR. The period of time in which it gives Blogs Engineering to respond is 14 days. What is deemed to be a reasonable period of time to reply will depend on the circumstances. In many straightforward debt claims 14 days is ample, but, where the facts are rather more complicated, it could be as much as 28 days.

14 February XXXX

Mr Fred Blogs
Finance Director
Blogs Engineering Limited

Dear Mr Blogs

LETTER BEFORE CLAIM
We write to you in respect of a proposed claim by Excellent Recruitment Limited against you for non-payment of our invoices rendered for services provided.

Pre-Action Protocol:
This letter is written in line with Annex A of the Practice Direction on Pre-Action Conduct where no specific protocol applies. As it would appear you are not legally represented, we enclose a copy of this Practice Direction. We draw attention to paragraph 4 concerning the court's powers to impose sanctions for failure to comply with the Practice Direction.

The Claim:
In August 2013, you approached Excellent Recruitment Ltd to recruit a secretary and also a quality control engineer. You spoke to our recruitment consultant, Fiona Rankin, and she sent you the terms and conditions which apply to our services. Ms Rankin put forward two candidates for the posts and you interviewed them both. You later engaged both candidates. We are claiming the total sum of £7,000 plus interest of £_____ and late payment compensation of £_____pursuant to the Late Payment of Commercial Debt (Interest) Act 1998 as amended). This is comprised of invoice 123 for £3,000 and invoice 124 for £4,000. Invoice 123 is for the recruitment of Jane Smith (a secretary) who commenced work on 4 September 2013 and invoice 124 is for the recruitment of Bill Jones who commenced work on 5 September 2013. The terms of payment were 14 days from the date of the invoices and so these invoices are due for payment but remain unpaid. We are not aware of a valid reason why payment has not been made.

Documents on which the Claimant intends to rely include:
All e-mail and other correspondence, invoices 123 and 124 (copies enclosed), Terms of Business sent on 10 August 2013 (a copy of these Terms are enclosed).

Time for a Response:
We believe it is reasonable for you to respond in full to this letter within **14 days of the date of this letter.**

Alternative Dispute Resolution (ADR):
We are willing to consider ADR to resolve this matter.

Payment:
Payment should be made by way of bank transfer to the following account:

Bank:	Good Interest Bank Plc
Account:	Excellent Recruitment
A/C No:	12345678
Sort Code:	11-00-99

If you ignore this letter before claim, it may lead to us starting court *proceedings and may increase your liability for costs.*

Yours sincerely

John Pride
Credit Manager
Excellent Recruitment

"Without Prejudice" letters - using them correctly

In the process of trying to negotiate a settlement of a claim, you may want to consider some form of compromise in order to "do a deal". In order to ensure that these compromises are not regarded as admissions where a deal cannot be achieved, one needs to properly utilise the words (or heading) "without prejudice"; this will mean that the contents therein cannot be used as evidence against you if the matter proceeds to court. However, "without prejudice" is commonly misunderstood and misused amongst laypeople. Simply putting the label "without prejudice" on a letter is not enough; the correspondence needs to be an attempt to settle a dispute. So, if a debtor replies to a letter of claim and heads it "without prejudice" and goes on to dispute the claim without actually discussing attempts to settle the case, then that would not be a correct use of the term "without prejudice".

If a letter is headed "without prejudice" and it contains threats or unequivocal admissions then the contents of the letter will not be protected. So, for example, if a debtor wrote a letter saying "*I admit that the debt is due but won't pay the debt and will go bankrupt*", then that would not be covered by the "without prejudice" rule. The correct use of "without prejudice" is where you are thinking that perhaps your case has some weaknesses and, therefore, you would be prepared to accept a compromise; however, you do not want that willingness to accept a lower figure to be regarded as an admission. An example of a "without prejudice" letter is shown below in the case of **Greenfield Housing Association and Hard Drive Computers**.

> *Greenfield Housing Association ("GHA") is in dispute with Hard Drive Computers "HDC") concerning a new accounts package they installed. Correspondence has passed between the parties. GHA maintain that they have suffered a loss because of the negligence of HDC when installing the new accounts package. GHA is claiming that they have suffered a loss of £7,000 in respect of additional*

costs to recover the lost data. HDC deny that they are responsible for the losses but, in an attempt to try and resolve the dispute quickly and salvage the business relationship, they write the following letter.

To: Greenfield Housing Association

Dear Sirs,

WITHOUT PREJUDICE – save as to costs

We feel disappointed that this dispute has reached the point of litigation. Our two organisations have had a long relationship over the last 10 years and do not want business dealings to end because of a disagreement over an unfortunate loss of data. While we understand the inconvenience the loss of data has caused, we do not accept that it was the fault of our IT engineers. However, to avoid this dispute dragging on, we are willing to offer, without admission of liability, the sum of £3,500 in full and final settlement of your claim for damages of £7,000.

Yours faithfully,

Steve Bolt
Hard Drive Computers

So it can be seen that Hard Drive Computers are not admitting the claim of Greenfield Housing, but for commercial reasons they would rather pay something than spend further time and money and risk having to pay out the whole sum claimed if they lost at court.

If the offer to settle is not accepted then the Defendant cannot use any concessions contained within the without prejudice as evidence in court. If Greenfield Housing were to accept the without prejudice offer, the parties would be bound by it. So if Hard Drive Computers were to go back on the deal then the agreement would be enforceable and the without prejudice correspondence could be relied upon to show the terms of the agreement.

The words "save as to costs" means that at the end of the trial the letter can be considered if the court has to consider the issue of costs. If the words "save as to costs" were not used, then - strictly speaking - the letter could not be relied upon when costs are discussed.

SUMMARY

Always attempt to try and resolve a dispute by using alternative methods. Alternative dispute resolution (ADR) can be a variety of methods, not simply mediation; attempting to have discussions with the other party is a form of ADR. The type of ADR which may be appropriate will depend on the size and nature of the claim. Before commencing legal action, write an appropriate pre-action letter that is in line with the court rules on pre-action conduct. The pre-action letter should set out your claim in sufficient detail so the Defendant can understand the nature of your claim and should enclose or refer to relevant documents. This letter of claim should always mention that you are willing to consider ADR. Attempts to try and resolve a dispute should be ongoing and so a court hearing should not necessarily be regarded as inevitable.

Chapter 2

ISSUING A CLAIM

Going to court should be regarded as the *last* resort when all efforts to settle have failed. You should remember the "no costs" rule in the small claims court, which means that you will only be able to recover the costs on the Claim Form. There are some limited situations where legal costs might be awarded, such as where a party has conducted their case in an unreasonable manner. This is referred to as "costs for unreasonable behaviour". The winning party may also be able to claim a small fixed amount for witness expenses and an expert's report if the court directed that it was necessary to have one.

Are you within time to make your claim?

There are time limits in which to bring legal claims. The Limitation Act 1980 sets out the different limitation periods depending on the type of claim. For example, in claims arising out of a breach of contract, a claim should be brought within six years of the breach of contract. In some contractual claims, the limitation period is twelve years if the contract was made under deed. In a claim based on tort, the limitation period is usually six years. However, in claims involving personal injury the limitation period is three years.

If you bring your claim outside the limitation period, it is open for the Defendant to raise the issue of limitation as a defence to the action.

Enforcement proceedings, i.e. steps taken after Judgment to collect your money, are not subject to any limitation period. A Judgment remains enforceable without a time limit. However, there may be some consequences of delaying enforcement. If enforcement proceedings are brought more than six years after Judgment then the interest that can be claimed is limited to that which has accrued over the six-year period. Permission is required to issue a writ so that an enforcement agent/bailiff can enforce a Judgment which is more than six years old. The court will take into account the delay when considering granting permission. Other forms of enforcement, such as charging orders and third party debt orders, do not require permission when seeking to enforce them more than six years after the Judgment. However, a Judgment debtor could seek to challenge enforcement methods if they can show there is compelling evidence of prejudice to the Judgment debtor from the delay in taking enforcement.

The strength of your claim

In taking court action, you have Judged that there is a reasonable prospect of success. What is a reasonable prospect of success? A reasonable prospect, in strict terms, means that you have a 51%, or better, chance of succeeding.   Trying to predict the prospects of success in percentage terms is not easy. Lawyers will, rightly, shy away from committing themselves in percentage terms. The chances of winning a case can often change over time as more evidence emerges. It is unusual for a barrister to state the merits of claim as being anything higher than 65% and, even when they *do* advise the merits as being around 60 to 65%, they will always give a warning of the uncertainty of court action and, consequently,   you may not get the result you expect.

Although it could be said that percentage prospects in the bracket of 51 to 60% are "reasonable prospects", many legal expenses insurers will not offer cover unless the chances of winning are at least 60%. From experience, even a case that - on paper - would be regarded as having a high percentage chance of success, there will be a number of occasions when the court hearing does not goes as well as you would like, with the evidence not being presented in the best light or the Judge taking an unexpected view of the evidence. So, from looking like you had an invincible case, it can easily fall apart and the case can be lost. The only sure thing is that you must be realistic when considering the prospects of success, and, it is wise to accept that the unexpected could happen rather than look around for somebody to blame if things go wrong.

The burden of proof

To succeed in a civil claim you have to prove your claim on the balance of probability. This is a phrase that you may have heard before, but what does it mean in practical terms? The balance of probability means "more likely than not". If it is more likely than not that your version of events is true, then the decision should go in your favour. There is a different standard of proof in criminal courts. In criminal courts, the standard of proof is "beyond reasonable doubt", which is a higher level of proof.

Does your opponent have the money to pay?

In addition to assessing the prospects of success, you should consider if your opponent has the means to pay if you get Judgment. There is little point in going the through the process of obtaining a Judgment and then not being able to recover the money awarded. However, there may be situations where you want to obtain a Judgment and sit on it for a few years until the debtor is in a better financial position when you will be able to enforce the Judgment. An example of this is where you are seeking a Judgment against a - currently impecunious - student but in a few years time he/she may be applying for their first mortgage and they are likely to be keen to settle any County Court Judgment to improve their chances of receiving a mortgage offer.

Although there is no limitation period in respect of enforcing a Judgment, there may be some circumstances where the Judgment debtor will try and challenge enforcement on the basis of delay, but central to that argument is the extent of prejudice to the debtor caused by the delay, and there must be compelling evidence of prejudice. It will be rare for a Judgment debtor to mount a successful challenge but you should bear in mind the possibility. As we live in times when people are more informed, you can expect people to try most things if they can avoid paying a Judgment.

Now that we are living in the Internet age, it is very easy to quickly obtain credit information about businesses. Acquiring information about the credit position of an individual is not so easy without their consent but there are still some basic checks that can be undertaken concerning an individual that do not cost much and do not require their consent. Simple checks on an individual such as searching the Register of County Court Judgments to see if there are any existing Judgments against that individual can be done online for a few pounds. You can also search the Land Registry to see if they own the address you have for the Defendant. In addition, an online search at the Insolvency Service website will reveal if an individual is currently bankrupt or subject to IVA (Individual Voluntary Arrangement). Of course, if the debt you are claiming arose before an insolvency order was made then you will not be able to pursue the debt; you would have to put a claim into the Official Receiver, or the appointed Trustee, in the hope that there might some distribution from any realisations made in relation to the Insolvency.

Checks on a business can be done through online credit checking facilities. A comprehensive credit report can be obtained quite cheaply and it will provide very valuable information as to whether or not you are likely to recover your money. A credit report on a company may provide, amongst other things:

- Overall net asset figure
- Any registered CCJ's
- Limited accounts information (Balance sheet).

Here is an example of a credit report that can easily be obtained online in a few minutes:

Comprehensive Report on - Green & Pleasant Land (UK) Management Ltd

CREDIT STATUS ANALYSIS

First Report Credit Limit: £7,000

SUMMARY

Registered Number:	000023331	**Sales:**	-
Date Incorporated:	19 August 2000	**Pre-Tax Profit/Loss:**	-
Date Latest Accounts:	31 July 2012	**Working Capital:**	£41,897
Employees:	-	**Net Assets:**	£51,253

Delphi Risk Score (1-100) 82

A low risk company; no reason to doubt credit transactions to the limit assigned.

BUSINESS INFORMATION

Legal Form:	Private Limited
Previous Names:	Greensite Management Ltd
Registered Number:	03259200
Annual Return:	30 September 2012
Registered Office:	10 Market Place, Uptown, Marketshire
Telephone Number:	-
Auditors:	Dodds and Co
SIC Code and Operations:	7032 (1992) MANAGE REAL ESTATE, FEE OR CONTRACT
PROPERTY MANAGEMENT.	
Parent Company:	-
Ultimate Parent:	-

PRINCIPAL SHAREHOLDERS

Fred Blogs - 10 £1 Ord Shares

DIRECTORS

Mr Fred Blogs

Mrs Valerie Smith

County Court Judgments

Period of Months:	Last 12m	13-24m	25-72m
Total Number of CCJs:	1	1	0
Total Value of CCJs:	£65	£80	£0

Date	Court	Amount	Status
July 2013	NORTHAMPTON	£65	Judgment
June 2012	NORTHAMPTON	£80	Judgment

Legal Notices / Filing History

None Recorded

SUPPLIER CREDIT LIMITS

Date	Sector	Notified	Amount	Terms
Nov-2010	Financial Services	Credit Limit	£2,000	30 days
Jan-2009	IT and Internet	Credit Limit	£500	30 days
Sep-2007	Construction	Credit Limit	£5,000	30 days

Supplier credit limit data is third party data taken on good faith and presented without comment or review.

PROFIT AND LOSS

Date of Accounts	31/07/12	31/07/11	31/07/10	31/07/09	31/07/08
Number of Weeks	52	52	52	52	52
Denomination	£	£	£	£	£
Turnover (Sales excluding VAT)	-	-	-	-	1,101,102
Cost of Sales (Raw materials, production costs etc.)	-	-	-	-	137,283
Gross Profit (Margin on production)	-	-	-	-	963,819
Operating Costs (Overheads, staff etc.)	-	-	-	-	924,332
Interest Payable (Bank and loan interest paid)	-	-	-	-	157
Pre-Tax Profit/(Loss) (Gross profit less operating costs etc.)	-	-	-	-	39,330
Taxation and Dividends	-	-	-	-	49,020
Retained Profit/(Loss) (Profit or loss after tax and dividends)	-	-	-	-	(9,690)

BALANCE SHEET

Date of Accounts	31/07/12	31/07/11	31/07/10	31/07/09	31/07/08
Number of Weeks	52	52	52	52	52
Denomination	£	£	£	£	£
Tangible Assets (Buildings, plant, vehicles etc.)	9,356	11,727	17,432	23,050	11,215
Intangible Assets (Patents, goodwill etc.)	0	0	0	0	0
Other Fixed Assets	0	0	0	0	0
Total Fixed Assets	9,356	11,727	17,432	23,050	11,215
Stocks & Work in Progress (Raw materials and order-book etc.)	37,950	1,200	1,200	1,200	1,200
Debtors (Cash due for work already done)	396,551	431,429	332,231	314,094	163,787
Cash (Cash already at bank and in hand)	14,668	23,274	21,966	14,667	55,378
Other Current Assets	0	0	0	0	0
Total Current Assets	449,169	455,903	355,397	329,961	220,365

The report on Green & Pleasant Land (UK) Management Ltd[4] shows a good credit score and a healthy positive net asset figure. There are a couple of small CCJ's against it but, in light of the overall net asset figure, these are not significant. Whilst such a credit report is useful information, a high credit score or a good credit level may, sometimes, be misleading and so, to interpret what these figures actually mean, you should consult someone who properly understands them. Such reports are a good initial guide as to the financial status of the company. If you see a report of a company, which has very little in the way of assets and many large unsatisfied CCJ's, then the chances are that the company is about to collapse.

Have all your information ready before you issue a claim and comply with court deadlines

From April 2013, various changes were made to the court rules. This followed a report by Lord Jackson. Many of his changes affect larger claims and costs management. However, one aspect that you should take very seriously before commencing legal action is to ensure that you meet any deadlines set by the court. There is a new, much tougher, attitude to those who do not meet a court deadline. If you are required to do something, e.g. file the Directions Questionnaire, by a particular date - and the court says if you do not do so the claim will be struck out - you will find it very difficult to succeed in an application for "relief from sanctions" (in this case ask for the claim to be instated) unless you can show a very good reason and you make an application very promptly.

The best way to ensure that you do not miss deadlines is to have all your paperwork, documents and witness statements ready before you issue a claim so as to avoid a last minute scramble to get the document(s) sent to the court, and the other side, on time. It is a very sensible approach to take when making a claim to ensure that you have gathered together the documents and evidence needed to prove your case prior to issuing court action. What can, sometimes, happen in legal matters brought by inexperienced laypeople is that they believe they have the basic elements of a claim but have not thought about the finer points of their case and what the other side may say in response before they embark on taking action. It is dangerous to use legal action, including small claims, as a sort of 'fishing expedition' to gauge any reaction you may get from the Defendant. You should have details of your claim prepared, accompanied by consideration supporting the contents of the

---

[4] Green & Pleasant Land (UK) Management Ltd is a fictitious company.

statement(s) therein, together with documents that you will use to prove your case *before* you start proceedings. It is prudent to anticipate any possible stance adopted by the Defendant and attempt to construct your statements accordingly. Witness evidence should be what the witness remembers as to the events surrounding the claim. There may be some comment on matters raised in the defence but the best statements are simply a factual account of what happened.

Putting together your case

Whether you are the Claimant or the Defendant, which is party to a small claim, you will need to support what you say with evidence. There are various forms of evidence:

- **Witnesses** - Individuals who have direct personal knowledge of the relevant facts and events.
- **Documents** - For example a written contract or correspondence.
- **Physical objects** - Damaged items that might be of importance. For example, in a consumer claim, to show that the article was defective.
- **Expert evidence** - An example might be a report to show that the trader, providing a service, did not exercise reasonable care and skill in performing the service; for example, work done by a garage.

Starting the claim
CCMCC or MCOL ?

If the claim you are going to make is for a sum of money then there are two methods to commence court action. There is the option of using "Money Claim Online" (MCOL), or, if you want to issue it on paper then you can post the Claim Form to the "County Court Money Claims Centre" (CCMCC), in Salford. You can no longer commence a claim for money by sending or taking a Claim Form to your local County Court. The CCMCC, in Salford, is a large administrative centre that deals with the early stages of new claims. Claims that become defended are transferred to the appropriate County Court for a hearing. There are some pros and cons associated with either method; using MCOL is convenient as you can sit at your computer and complete the forms online. However, the space provided for the particulars of claim on MCOL is quite limited. There is the option to prepare separate particulars of claim which you can send to the Defendant and the court within 14 days, but experience suggests that there is quite a delay and an element of difficulty in matching up paperwork to the court file. Therefore, if you are going to use MCOL then it is best to do so where you can fit the particulars of claim into the 1,088-character allowance provided. A claim, such as a very simple unpaid bill for goods delivered, would be an appropriate one for MCOL, where the claim has been admitted or is - highly unlikely - to involve a dispute. There is the advantage, when using MCOL, that the court fees are slightly lower and one is able make payment of the court fee online by using a credit or debit card.

The CCMCC, in Salford, opened during March 2012. It was designed to deal with the early stages of money claims. Although the issuing of proceedings through the CCMCC may take rather longer, as opposed to one using their local County Court, and, the issue fees are slightly higher than MCOL, and where the claim is rather more involved and includes contractual documents which you need to refer to in the particulars of claims, it is better to issue through Salford than MCOL.

The one big disadvantage that is experienced with both MCOL and CCMCC is that, if you need to speak to them on the telephone or get in touch by letter to follow up the issuing of a claim, it can take a long time to get through on the call centre number and it can take a while to get a response by post. Perhaps the best way to communicate with CCMCC and MCOL is by e-mail, as this seems to generate a reply slightly quicker.

To start the claim using MCOL, you need to visit:
www.**moneyclaim**.gov.uk

The claim has to be for a monetary amount that is less than £100,000. You have to pay for the court fees by credit or debit card. Users of this system cannot obtain an exemption from court fees. The service is open to individuals, solicitors and companies. It operates 24 hours a day, 7 days a week and so you can go online anytime and monitor the progress of your case.

Setting out your claim

The following assumes that you are going to use CCMCC. The claim is, therefore, more than a simple undisputed debt claim. The issuing of a claim should involve very careful preparation of the nature of your claim because, if the information is incorrect then, without the consent of the Defendant, you are going to need to make an application to the court for permission to amend the particulars of your claim. Such an application will require a court fee.

Before sitting down to write the particulars of your claim, think about the basis on which you claim is to be made. In law, your claim must have a "cause of action". The layperson may have a good general knowledge of some of the basic concepts; such as a small business suing a customer for non-payment of a debt (a breach of contract). A person who has had their car damaged through the fault of another driver will probably understand that the claim is based on negligence. In straightforward cases, such as a rear end shunt or where a car pulls out in front of you, it is usually quite simple to establish that the Defendant has been negligent in that he has failed to drive to the standard expected of a reasonable driver. The reasonable driver should drive with sufficient distance between him and the car in front to enable him to slow/stop safely, and without a collision, in the event that the car in front has to slow down or stop. Therefore, in virtually all cases of a rear end shunt, if you go into the back of the vehicle in front, you will almost certainly be to blame.

In other cases, the claim may be based on certain consumer rights. Most consumers will know that the Sale of Goods Act 1979, as amended, gives them certain rights if the goods they purchase from a retailer are not of satisfactory quality.

There will be times when the basis of your claim may not be so obvious or, when considering the circumstances, you are not sure whether the facts are sufficient to establish the claim you are thinking of bringing. In these situations - and especially where the claim is in the upper end of the small claims limit - it is highly advisable to pay for some legal advice. You may begrudge paying a lawyer a few hundred pounds or so for an initial assessment of your case, but you may live to regret that decision later after having paid court fees in excess of this and not being able to recover those fees because you made some fundamental mistakes over the cause of action. It is true that the small claims track is a less formal process and District Judges will do all they can to ensure you understand the process and get a fair hearing, but they cannot simply ignore the law if you blatantly do not have a valid cause of action.

Interest, Late Payment Compensation and reasonable collection costs for commercial debts

The changes to the Late Payment Regulations that came into force on 16 March 2013[5] provide an avenue for businesses to recover some of its collection costs when it is chasing an overdue business debt. The Late Payment Regulations were initially introduced by the Late Payment of Commercial Debt (Interest) Act 1998 and were followed by some amendments within Regulations formed by Statutory Instruments. An

---

[5] The Late Payment of Commercial Debt Regulations 2013; SI 2013 No 395

Act of Parliament will often contain "enabling provisions", which provide for the Government to make changes to an Act at a later date by passing Statutory Instruments rather than passing a completely new Act of Parliament. The Late Payment of Commercial Debts Regulations 2013 implemented the European Directive 2011/7/EU on combating late payment in commercial transactions and aims to make pursuing payment a simpler process across the European Union, thereby reducing the culture of paying late and, instead, making payment on time the norm.

Under these Late Payment Regulations, if you are a business involved in a commercial transaction with another business, they must pay your invoice within 60 days, unless expressly agreed otherwise and provided it is not unfair to the creditor. The statutory interest rate of 8 percentage points above the Bank of England's reference rate applies to the debt unless an agreement has been reached which amounts to a substantial remedy for the late payment of the debt.

How to calculate late payment interest:

The reference rate is set at the start of each six-month period, which is the Bank of England's base rate, and this will apply for the following six months. To obtain the correct rate of interest under the Late Payment Regulations, all you need to do is add 8% per cent to the reference rate that covers the period in which your debt became late. To calculate the amount of simple interest (not compound interest) apply this formula:

$$\frac{\text{Debt x interest rate x number of days late}}{365}$$

Late payment compensation

As well being entitled to interest arising from late payment, suppliers will also be able to claim a fixed amount of "compensation" depending on the size of the unpaid debt. The table below shows how much you are entitled to claim.

Amount of unpaid debt	Amount of fixed compensation
£0-£999.99	£40
£1,000 - £9,999.99	£70
£10,000 and over	£100

Reasonable collection costs

The Late Payment Regulations, introduced on 16 March 2013, provided for the recovery of reasonable collection costs where the costs of collection exceed the fixed level of compensation set out above. The 2013 Regulations introduced the following to the 1998 Act:

> "(2A) If the reasonable costs of the supplier in recovering the debt are not met by the fixed sum, the supplier shall also be entitled to a sum equivalent to the difference between the fixed sum and those costs."

For guidance on what is included by the words "reasonable collection costs", look at Article 6 of European Directive 2011/7/EU, which is the Directive which is implemented by the 2013 Regulations. Article 6 states:

> 3.   The creditor shall, in addition to the fixed sum referred to in paragraph 1, be entitled to obtain reasonable compensation from the debtor for any recovery costs exceeding that fixed sum and incurred due to the debtor's late payment. This could include expenses incurred, inter alia, in instructing a lawyer or employing a debt collection agency.

So it is clear that "reasonable collection" costs include the expenses incurred in instructing a lawyer or employing a debt collection agency. This is useful for businesses chasing a commercial debtor where the creditor incurs legal costs in collecting a debt that exceed the fixed compensation rates. Suppose, for example, a business is chasing another company for an unpaid account of say £8,000 and the creditor decides to employ a debt collection agency followed by a lawyer to send a formal pre-action protocol letter as well draft the Particulars of Claim. The fixed compensation in this case is £70 but it is more than likely that the costs of the debt collection agency and that of the lawyer will exceed £70. If we assume that the debt collection costs and legal costs are £500, then the creditor will be able to claim reasonable collection costs above the £70 of £430. The collection costs would be awarded unless they were deemed unreasonable.

The provisions of the Regulations could be at odds with the Civil Procedure Rules. As will be examined in more detail later, when we consider what costs can be claimed in small claims, the general position under the Civil Procedure Rules, Part 27, is that the only costs that can be awarded are certain fixed costs and, potential, additional costs where it can be shown that a party has behaved unreasonably in the conduct of the case.

Completing the Claim Form (N1)

Part 16 of the Civil Procedure Rules and the accompanying Practice Direction set out certain matters that need to be included in the Claim Form (Form "N1"). An example of a completed Claim Form is among the forms shown in Appendix A. It would be worth familiarising yourself with this section of the rules before preparing your claim. A layperson cannot be expected to know every aspect of the rules and it would serve no purpose in going through every item, but it would help to be aware of some of important sections that relate to a Claim Form:

1. The Claim Form must include an address at which the Claimant resides or carries on business. This applies even if the Claimant's solicitor is accepting service of court documents.

2. Where the Defendant is an individual, the Claim Form should, if able to do so, include an address at which the Defendant resides or carries on business.

3. The address given must include a postcode. If a postcode is not given, the court will issue the claim but not serve it until the full postcode is supplied.

4. The Claim Form must be headed with the full names of the parties. In the case of an individual, it is the title and full name by which he/she is known:

Mr Brian Alfred Jones

If the individual is carrying on business in a name other than his own name, his full name and that of the full trading name should used:

Mr Brian Alfred Jones, trading as "BJ Motors".

In the case of a partnership, other than a Limited Liability Partnership, the full name by which the partnership is known followed by the words "A Firm" should be used. In the case of a limited liability company or limited liability partnership registered in England and Wales, you should state the full registered name followed by the suffix "plc", Limited", "Ltd", or "LLP".

5. The Claim Form must contain a statement of value. It will either state the value of the claim, that the amount claimed will not exceed £10,000, or the Claimant cannot say how much is likely to be recovered. In a claim which includes a claim by a tenant of residential premises against a landlord, where the tenant is seeking an order requiring the landlord to carry out repairs or other work to the premises, the Claimant must also state in the Claim Form whether the estimated costs of those repairs or other work is –

(i) Not more than £1,000; or

(ii) More than £1,000; and

(b) Whether the value of any other claim for damages is –

(i) Not more than £1,000; or

(ii) More than £1,000.

6. On the front page, state your preferred court for hearings. Try and be specific about the court where you prefer any court hearings.

7. On the second page, state whether the claim involves any human rights issues, which - in most small claims - the answer will be "No".

8. On the second page there is a section where you can write the particulars of claim. If you cannot fit the particulars into this box then you can write "see attached" and set them out on a separate sheet. The particulars of claim should be a concise statement of your claim.

The importance of ensuring you have named and described the Defendant correctly cannot be overstated. More times than I can remember, I have seen the Defendant incorrectly described and on many occasions the legal entity is incorrect. If you simply state "Blogs Motors" then that is *not* a legal entity. It will either be:

- Blogs Motors Limited (if it is a limited company)
- Blogs Motors (A Firm) if it is a partnership, or
- Fred Blogs t/a "Blogs Motors" if Mr Blogs is the sole proprietor

If you obtained a court Judgment with the wrong party or legal entity named on it then, when you come to enforce it, you will be mightily embarrassed when the bailiff reports back to you that he could not enforce the Judgment because the Defendant does not exist. Although it is possible to bring a claim against the trading name of a business, provided you can show it is clear who the Defendant is, it is much better to state the right legal entity. If you get a Judgment against Fred Blogs t/a Blogs Motors, when in fact it should have been "Blogs Motors Ltd", the Defendant will happily remind the bailiff that the goods he is eager to seize are in fact owned by the company - not him personally!

Whilst – in the event that you get things wrong on the Claim Form - you can make amendments, you need to be aware that if it has been deemed as being served upon the Defendant, by the court, then you would have to make an application to the court for permission to amend if the other party does not consent to the desired changes being made. That will cost a further court fee and you may incur legal costs if the other side has to make changes to their statement of case as a result. So, whilst ensuring that you are suing the right person/company may seem obvious, all too often this aspect is not given sufficient thought at the right time, which is before you start a claim and not once you are well down the litigation road. In business, it is important that you train sales staff who get customers to complete order forms to ensure they get the right information, so it is clear from the start who you are contracting with.

The box marked "particulars of claim" on the Claim Form is where you enter a concise statement of your case. If you cannot fit the details of you claim into this space on the Claim Form, attach a separate sheet but it is usual to head the attached sheet as follows:

In the County Court Money Claims Centre   *Case No_____*

Between

XXXXXXXXXXXXXX   *Claimant*

And

YYYYYYYYYYYYYYY   *Defendant*

Particulars of Claim

The drafting of the particulars of claim is not an easy exercise for the layperson. Some laypeople think is it just a case of attaching/referring to every piece of correspondence and all documents connected with the case; this is *not* the way to draft your claim. It is not unusual for litigants in person to include every item of evidence in their particulars of claim but there is a difference between what goes into the particulars of claim and evidence. A simple way of explaining what should go in the statement of case (or "pleading" as they have traditionally been known) is to look at some typical examples. In the case of a road traffic accident, your particulars of claim will concisely state:

1. On _____ at approx. _____ the Claimant was driving a vehicle registration number _____ along Market Road, in Upton when a vehicle driven by the Defendant collided into the Claimant's vehicle causing damage to the Claimant's vehicle.

2. The Claimant claims that the Defendant was negligent in that:

– drove out from a side road into the path of the Claimant's vehicle

– failed to keep a proper look out

– failed to give way to the Claimant who had right of way

– failed to take any or any reasonable steps to avoid to a collision

3. As a result of the Defendant's negligence, the Claimant suffered loss and damage to his vehicle.

4. The Claimant claims the cost of repairs to his vehicle and the cost of hiring a vehicle while his vehicle was being repaired.

All the evidence to support the allegation that the Defendant was negligent will come later in the witness statements and other documentation. The witness statement of the Claimant might say; *"I was driving along Market Road on xx/xx/xx within the speed limit when from the left hand side a vehicle came out into the path of my car. The driver of the other vehicle was looking in the other direction as he pulled out from the junction with Spencer Lane..."* etc.

What the above example of a road traffic accident claim, hopefully, shows is the difference between the statement of case and evidence. The statements of case set out the legal nature of the claim, in this case negligence, whereas the evidence in the form of witness statements and other documentation is the evidence to support the allegations of negligence.

The following is an example of a breach of contract claim. The key to setting out a claim for breach of contract is to:

1. Identify the parties to the contract.
2. State whether the contract was written or oral (or both).
3. Identify the key terms and attach a copy of the written contract if there is one.
4. Give details of the term(s) of the contract which has/have been breached.
5. State your loss as a result of the breach of contract.

1.The Claimant is a writer. The Defendant was acting in the course of business as a book publisher.

2. The Defendant entered into a written contract with the Claimant on xx/xx/xx, a copy which is attached, to proof read and print 1,000 copies of the Claimant's novel for an agreed price of £_____ which the Claimant paid in advance. The express terms of the Contract included:

– The 1,000 printed books be delivered to the Claimant by the Defendant by no later than xx/xx/xx.
– The Defendant should read the manuscript to correct typing errors.

There were also implied terms into the contract that the book would be of satisfactory quality and fit for purpose.

3. The Defendant was in breach of the express and implied Terms of the contract because:
– The books were delivered 3 months after the agreed delivery date.
– The book contained a substantial number of uncorrected typing errors.
– The book was not of satisfactory quality.

4. As result of the Defendant's breach of contract, the Claimant has suffered a loss and claims the return of monies paid and/or damages, plus interest in accordance with section 69 of the County Courts Act 1984.

The above example demonstrates the nature of the claim in that the

Claimant contracted with the Defendant to proof read and print his latest manuscript. There were express terms as to the delivery date and for the correction of typing errors. The Defendant did not deliver the book on time and it contained many uncorrected typing errors.

The two examples given as to how to draft simple particulars of claim are relatively straightforward cases. However, if your case involves complicated facts or difficult points of law then it would make sense to spend some money on a lawyer to set out your claim properly. Even if you do not instruct your lawyer to act throughout the claim, spending some money at the start to set out the case where it is not a straightforward claim will be well worth it in the long run. If you have particulars of claim that are not clear then the other side is going to enjoy taking it apart in the Defence. If it is very badly drafted then it is possible it could be struck out or the District Judge may request that you provide further information under CPR Part 27.2(3).

Once you have completed the Claim Form, you need to send to the court:

- The original Claim Form
- A copy of the Claim Form for each Defendant
- Payment of the court fee. Court fees for issuing money claims can be found on the Court Service website and are set out in Appendix A (prices correct as at the time of publishing).

On receiving the Claim, the court will issue a case number and send the copy to the Defendant. You will receive a Notice of Issue from the court that will confirm the date when the claim was issued, the date it was served (i.e. sent to the Defendant) and the deemed date of service (the date when the Defendant is deemed to have received the Claim Form). The court rules state that the date when a claim is deemed to have been served on the Defendant (received by the Defendant) is the second day after it was posted provided that day is a business day; if not, the next business day after that.

It is advisable to allow the court to serve the Claim Form on the Defendant. If you do it, you will have to enclose the response pack and then file a certificate of service at the court to prove that service on the Defendant has been done. Best to avoid this further work unless, for example, you don't have an address for the Defendant and you are going to have to consider personal service. If you do decide to serve it on the Defendant yourself then you need to make that clear in the covering letter to the court. In which case, they will return a sealed copy of the Claim Form (sealed means with the court's stamp on it) and the response pack used by the Defendant to respond to the claim.

The Business Centre at Salford processes all paperwork up until the claim becomes disputed. At that point, Salford will send out a Notice of Proposed Allocation along with the Directions Questionnaire. Upon receipt of the Directions Questionnaire from the Claimant and Defendant, it will transfer the case to the appropriate County Court hearing centre to list the case for a hearing and deal with any administration leading up to the trial.

SUMMARY

It is important that, before you issue your claim in the County Court, you should ensure that you have considered the strength of your claim and whether or not your opponent will have the money to pay if you succeed in obtaining Judgment. Before starting your claim, it would be worth spending some money on legal fees to ensure that you have set out the particulars of your claim in line with the court rules as well as presenting the case in the best way. This is important because, if you wish to amend the details *after* you have served a court claim then, unless your opponent agrees, you will have to make an application to the court for permission to amend. That will involve court fees and so it is best to get it right first time.

Chapter 3

The Defendant's Reply

When I say to a layperson that court proceedings have been issued, it is often assumed that the next stage is a court hearing. Whether or not a claim will go to a court hearing depends on the reply from the Defendant. The Defendant has fourteen days from the date the Claim is deemed served in which to respond. If the Claim Form is deemed served on the second of the month, the Defendant has until 4pm on the sixteenth of the month to get their reply to the court office. If the sixteenth is *not* a business day then the date for filing the reply at the court would be 4pm on the next business day. The Defendant should also send a copy of the defence to the Claimant. In order to have twenty-eight days from the date of service in which to file the defence at court, the Defendant can send the Acknowledgment of Service to the court within fourteen days indicating an intention to defend the claim. The Acknowledgment of Service form (N9) is shown in Appendix A.   Consideration has been given to abolishing the Acknowledgment of Service form as it is regarded as an administrative burden on the court process. If the Defendant requires longer than 28 days to complete and file his defence, then he can either seek the consent of the Claimant for an extension of time or if they do not agree, apply to the court.

The parties to a claim can agree, without the permission of the court, to extend the date for filing a defence by up to 28 days. The extension of the time will run from the date when the defence was originally due. If the parties agree to extend the time limit for filing a defence they must inform the court before the original period expires. Where the Defendant is a company or the individual has a solicitor acting, it is common for him to contact the Claimant for an extension of time in which to file the defence. Your first reaction will probably be to say "no" to such a request. It is common practice to allow one short extension of time if requested, for example 7 days. You do not have to agree to it. However, if the Defendant was unable to file a defence in time and you entered Judgment, he will probably make an application to set aside Judgment. If there is a defence with a realistic prospect of success, the District Judge will almost certainly set aside Judgment and would regard your refusal to grant extra time as unreasonable conduct.

The Defendant may respond to the Claim Form in one the following ways:

- Pay the whole claim.
- Admit the claim and make an offer to pay.
- Admit part of the claim.
- Dispute the claim and enter a defence.
- Ignore the claim.

On the filing of a defence to a claim, which does not exceed £10,000, the matter is usually allocated to the small claims track. The word "defence" includes when a Defendant admits liability but disputes the amount owed.

The parties to a claim can agree, without the permission of the court, to extend the period for filing a defence by up to twenty-eight days. The extension of the time will run from the date when the defence was originally due. If the parties agree to extend the time limit for filing a defence then they must inform the court before the original period expires. Where the Defendant is a company, or the individual has a solicitor acting, it is common for him to contact the Claimant for an extension of time in which to file the defence. Your first reaction will probably be to say no to such a request. It is common practice to allow one short extension of time if requested; for example, seven days. You do not have to agree to it. However, if the Defendant was unable to file a defence in time and you entered Judgment then he will probably make an application to set aside Judgment. If there is a defence with a realistic prospect of success then the District Judge will almost certainly set aside Judgment and would regard your refusal to grant extra time as unreasonable conduct.

Defendant admits your claim and makes offer to pay

If the Defendant admits your claim and offers to pay by instalments then what happens if you reject the offer? A court officer will decide a reasonable rate of payment and will notify both parties. Either party then has sixteen days in which he can apply for the rate of payment to be reconsidered by a District Judge. However, be prepared for the court to decide a low rate of payment - especially where the Defendant is an individual. Once the rate of payment has been set, a formal order is drawn up and sent to both parties. The Defendant is warned that if he does not pay the instalments as ordered then enforcement proceedings might be taken against him.

It is a well-known frustration of creditors that debtors are ordered to pay a small amount per month. In some cases, it takes many months - or even years - to pay off the debt. However, if you believe the debtor's finances have improved then you can apply to the court to vary the rate of payment.

If you accept the admission and the offer to pay then you can ask the court to enter Judgment on those terms. To enter Judgment, use the Notice of Issue form that contains a section at the bottom for requesting Judgment. If the Defendant admits part of the claim, you cannot request Judgment for the part they admit and pursue the balance. If you reject a part admission then it proceeds as a defended claim.

The Defendant, or his legal representative, may write a "without prejudice" letter offering to pay the claim on the condition that you withdraw court proceedings or do not request a Judgment. If you agree then you should take steps to protect your position in case the Defendant goes back on his promise. You would be well advised to draw up a simple "Tomlin Order". This is a type of consent order named after the case in which it was first used. The effect is that the court proceedings are stayed (suspended) except to enable the parties to refer the matter back to court for putting the agreed terms into effect. If you simply wrote to the court and asked for the action to be withdrawn and the Defendant failed to do as promised, you could not restart the court proceedings. By drawing up a consent order with the correct wording, you can proceed to enforce the agreed terms if the Defendant does not do as promised. To ask the Court to enter a Consent Order usually requires a court fee to be paid. The Consent Order should be worded as follows:

IN THE ....COUNTY COURT   CASE No.

Between:

.... (Claimant)

and

.... (Defendant)

TOMLIN ORDER

BY CONSENT

IT IS ORDERED THAT:

1. Upon the parties having agreed to the terms set forth in the schedule hereto, all further proceedings in this claim be stayed, except for the purpose of carrying such terms into effect. Liberty to apply to carry such terms into effect.

We agree to an Order on the above terms

Date:

Signed   _____   _____

          Claimant   Defendant

Schedule:

a. The Defendant shall pay the Claimant the sum of £3,000 by instalments of £500 per month with the first payment due on the 10th May 2____, and thereafter on the 10th day of each following month.

b. If the Defendant defaults on the terms set out in paragraph 1, the Claimant may request Judgment without further order of the Court.

The Defendant admits part of the claim

If the Defendant admits part of the claim then you are faced with whether you respond to the court to accept it or refuse the part admission. If you refuse the part admission, then the case continues as a defended matter.

The Defendant disputes your claim and enters a defence

To enter a defence, the Defendant should complete form N9b and send it to the court and a copy to the Claimant. The defence may come in the form of a separate document provided it complies with the court rules. In particular, the document should have the heading of the action and the claim number. At the end of the defence document, in the same way as the Claim Form, it must be verified by a "statement of truth". It is important to look and see if the defence contains a statement of truth.

On receiving the defence, you may wonder whether you should enter a reply. It is not a requirement to enter a reply. However, if the defence contains a counterclaim, you must enter a defence to the counterclaim otherwise a Judgment in default can be entered against you, in respect of the counterclaim, at the request of the Defendant.

A reply should only be prepared and filed at court if there are proper grounds to do so. A situation where a reply to the defence might be prepared is where the defence raises new issues not addressed in the Particulars of Claim. However, the reply should not be used as a method to amend your Particulars of Claim. If you wish to change the basis of your claim then you should seek to amend the Particulars of Claim. Bearing in mind that, if the Defendant does not consent to you amending your Particulars of Claim then you would need to make an application to the court, and with court fees having recently increased in respect of making an "on notice" application, you would probably wish to avoid seeking an amendment, because of the cost, and also consider whether the cost is proportional as it is a small claim. The reality is that lawyers often stretch the rules as to whether a reply should be an amendment to the Claim. However, as the formal rules of procedure are more relaxed in small claims, it is likely that the District Judge will simply want to have a clear picture as to what each party is saying, rather than being too concerned with the technical rules of setting out statements of case. Also, as a layperson, you will not be expected to understand these technical legal arguments.

If a Defence is entered then the court will usually allocate the claim to the small claims track if:

- The claim has a financial value of not more than £10,000 subject to the special provisions about claims for personal injuries and housing disrepair claims;
- The claim is for personal injuries which has a financial value of – not more than – £10,000 where the claim for damages for personal injuries is not more than £1,000; and
- any claim which includes a claim by a tenant of residential premises against his landlord for repairs or other work to the premises where the estimated cost of the repairs or other work is not more than £1,000 and the financial value of any other claim for damages is not more than £1,000)

If the above applies, the court will send out:

1. A notice provisionally allocating the case to the small claims track.
2. If not represented, the Directions Questionnaire (form N180) to complete and

return to court and a copy to the other side.

3. State any other requirements to be complied with.

A copy of the Directions Questionnaire is contained in the collection of court forms in Appendix A. The Directions Questionnaire for small claims requires very little information and some would say it is a pointless administrative exercise. Perhaps the only important question on the form is the first, which asks:

"Do you agree this claim should be referred to the small claims mediation service? Yes/No"

The small claims mediation service provided by the courts is conducted by telephone. It will involve the court mediator telephoning each party to try and assist the parties in reaching a settlement.

Although the Directions Questionnaire seems to be of little significance, you do need to complete it and send it back to the court. If you don't then the court will warn you and then, if you *still* have not completed and returned one, your claim will be struck out. Trying to restore a struck out claim is more difficult than it once was because the court now takes a different and stricter approach to an application for what is called "relief from sanctions". If you are asking the court to re-instate a struck out claim then what you are doing is asking for the court to exercise its discretion and reverse the particular sanction that has been imposed, in this situation the striking out of the claim. So the message is clear, if the court instructs you to do something by a particular date then you need to comply; otherwise you run the risk of having your case struck out and it will not be easy to get it re-instated.

After returning the Directions Questionnaire to the CCMCC in Salford, the claim will be transferred to the appropriate County Court hearing centre. If the Defendant is an individual, then it will automatically be transferred to the Defendant's home court. The District Judge at that County Court will look at the statements of case and give directions and list it for a hearing for an appropriate length of time, usually about 1 hour or 90 minutes. Small claims are rarely listed for longer than 2 hours.

If the Defence has little merit, do you apply for Summary Judgment?

If you receive a defence that has no real prospect of success, you may consider applying for Summary Judgment under CPR Part 24. This sounds perfectly logical if the defence appears to have no merit. However, in practice it may not achieve a great deal in respect of obtaining the Judgment sooner than if you had waited for the small claims hearing to be listed. There will be a court fee to be paid and the chances are the court may not be able to list the application much sooner than it would have done if you had waited for the full hearing. However, there is a fee to make the application which carries the risk of further expenditure wasted if you are not ultimately successful in your claim. If you can dispose of the case by way of Summary Judgment then the fee would be less - in most cases - than the hearing fee. So, there may be a small saving in court fees and you might arrive at decision slightly earlier. It is important that you are sure you have grounds for making an application. Under CPR Part 24.2; the court may give Summary Judgment if it considers that the Defendant has "no real prospect of successfully defending the claim" and that "there is no other compelling reason why the case should be disposed of at a trial". In the recent case of ***Ticketus LLP and another v. Whyte and others (2013)***, the court looked at the test for what is a "realistic prospect of success". It re-enforced the fact that the court must decide whether the Defendant has a "realistic" - as opposed to "fanciful" - prospect of success.

A 'realistic' defence is more than merely arguable. The court must not conduct a 'mini-trial' although this does not mean that the court should take the Defendant's statement of case at face value, particularly if contradicted by contemporaneous documents. The court should take into account the evidence before it, but also the evidence that can reasonably be expected to be available at trial. So the court might hesitate about making a final decision without a trial where reasonable grounds exist for believing that a fuller investigation into the facts of the case would alter the evidence available. If the court is satisfied that it has all the evidence necessary, for the proper determination of the issue in question and that the parties have had an adequate opportunity to put forward their arguments, then it should proceed to decide the case at the Summary Judgment hearing. It is not enough to argue that the case should be allowed to go to trial because something "may turn up".

In practice, where the Defendant is an unrepresented individual, it is likely that the court will give them the benefit of doubt and say that it is not satisfied that it has all the evidence necessary to determine the issues. On that basis, you may not want to apply for Summary Judgment unless there is very clear documentary evidence that the Defendant owes the money claimed.

The Defendant ignores the Claim Form

If the Defendant does not reply to your Claim Form within 14 days – or, after filing an acknowledgment of service within 14 days, then fails to file a defence within 28 days of the date of service of the claim - you can ask the court to enter 'Judgment in default'. The court will check their file to ensure that no response was received from the Defendant and then enter Judgment.

However, this Judgment may not be final. The Defendant may make an application to the court to set aside Judgment. If there was an error in the procedure then the Defendant may ask for the Judgment to be set aside as a right. An example of this would be where the court entered Judgment before the time for filing a defence had passed, or, if a defence had been filed in time but was not discovered by the court until after a Judgment had been entered. If the procedure was followed correctly, the Judge has discretion to set aside a Judgment entered in default where the Defendant has a real prospect of successfully defending the claim or there is some other good reason why the Defendant should be allowed to defend the claim.

It is not uncommon for a Defendant, faced with the Claimant taking steps to enforce the Judgment obtained in default, to make an application to set aside. If this happens to you then knowing the basis upon which the Defendant might succeed will not only avoid you worrying about the process but also enable you to assemble arguments against the application.

The civil rules in respect of the test for setting aside a Judgment state:

(1) In any case the court may set aside or vary a Judgment entered under Part 12 if:

(a) the Defendant has a real prospect of successfully defending the claim, or

(b) it appears to the court that there is some other good reason why:

(i) the Judgment should be set aside or varied, or

(ii) the Defendant should be allowed to defend the claim.

(2) In considering whether to set aside or vary a Judgment entered under Part 12, the matters to which the court must have regard include whether the person seeking to set aside the Judgment made an application to do so promptly.'

The court will look at whether the Defence has a real prospect of success. It is not enough for the Defendant to show an arguable Defence. The test is the same as in Summary Judgment application. The only difference is that the burden of proof is upon the Defendant in an application to set aside Judgment.

There is no definition as to what constitutes "some other good reason". It may be surprising that, where a Defendant did not receive notice of the Claim, he is not entitled as of right to the default Judgment being set aside if the claim was deemed served in accordance with the court rules. The Defendant would have to argue that the court should exercise it discretion as it is good reason why the Judgment should be set aside.

An issue that often arises is where a debtor makes application to set aside quite a long time after the Judgment was entered. Comments by Lord Justice Moore-Bick in the case of **Standard Bank Plc v Agrinvest International Inc. (2010)** make clear the importance of making an application to set aside promptly. Although this aspect was not part of the reason for decision in the case, the Lord Justice commented that he was not impressed by the explanation of why the Defendant had not made the application to set aside until March 2009, when there was evidence that he had acknowledged receipt of the Judgment in an e-mail dated 22nd February 2008.

Although making an application a long time after Judgment has been entered does not prevent the court from setting aside a Judgment (if there is a real prospect of the Defendant successfully defending), the court would expect a credible explanation of why there was a delay. There are no hard and fast rules about what is regarded as acting promptly, but a Defendant would normally have difficulty if he has delayed for a month, or more, before making the application.

SUMMARY

There are a number of potential responses that you may receive from the Defendant following the issuing of a claim. The Defendant might file a defence, admit the claim, admits part of the claim or may simply ignore the claim - enabling you to request Judgment in default. If the defence clearly raises new issues - not addressed in the Particulars of Claim - then you may wish to file a reply to the defence at the time you return the Directions Questionnaire to the court or within 14 days of receiving the defence. Even when you have obtained Judgment in default, there are circumstances where the Defendant can make an application to set aside Judgment provided he can show the court that there is a real prospect of successfully defending the claim, or, there is some other compelling reason why the Judgment should be set aside.

CHAPTER 4

Preparing For the Small Claims Hearing

Once you have filed the Directions Questionnaire, you will - in due course - receive a Notice of Hearing from the court which will contain the date of the trial and the Directions setting out what the parties have to do to prepare for the hearing.

From the point when the local County Court receives the papers after a Directions Questionnaire has been filed, it is likely that the small claims hearing will be listed for date that is about 3 to 4 months ahead. The length of time it takes to receive a hearing date will vary depending on how busy the court is. If a particular County Court has many cases ready for hearing then it is a matter of waiting for the next available slot in the court list. Where a District Judge is sits in more than one court, he may - at any time, upon application or upon his own motion, direct that the hearing shall take place in some other court of which he is a Judge. This can reduce the delay in a case receiving a hearing date.

The case will automatically be transferred to the Defendant's home court where the Defendant is not a company. If the case has been transferred to a court, which is a long distance away, then you can apply to a District Judge for the case to be heard at a more suitable venue; this application is made by putting your representations in writing to the District Judge. The District Judge decides the venue by considering the written submissions. However, it may take a while for the matter to go before a District Judge.

When a date for the small claims hearing is set, each party is sent a Notice of Small Claims Hearing; this form states that if a party objects to it being dealt with under the small claims procedure, then an application should be made to the court. A Defendant wishing to delay matters might decide to apply to the court to object to the case being dealt with by the small claims procedure. The court might fix an appointment before the District Judge to consider the objections.

Where the claim is for an unspecified sum, the case is not transferred automatically to the Defendant's home court. However, if there is an application to set aside Judgment in default then the case will be subject to automatic transfer.

The usual directions that will be sent out with the Notice will be:

At least 14 days before the hearing date:

- send to the other party and to the court a copy of all documents you are going to use to prove your case.

- send to the other party and to the court signed witness statements of any oral evidence to be given at the hearing. Witnesses include the parties to the action.

The court order giving the directions for a small claims hearing will make clear that if you do not comply with them then the District Judge may not allow you to rely on any documents or oral evidence at the hearing. Laypeople may think that because there is a less formal approach to evidence and procedure, they can be quite laid-back when they file and serve documents which they wish to rely on at the hearing. In my experience, District Judges are now becoming much less tolerant of parties (including laypeople) who do not send their bundle of documents for the hearing to the court and the other party by the deadline stated in the directions order. If you arrive at the hearing, wanting to rely on documents that you have not filed within the deadline, the Judge may adjourn if the other party argues they should not be allowed to use the documents because they have only recently been given copies. However, the Judge is quite likely to order costs to be paid by the party which caused the adjournment; this will include the other party's wasted costs and legal costs if they have legal representation. But don't assume the Judge will allow an adjournment - particularly if you had notice of the hearing with the directions many months before. In such situations, the Judge may proceed with the hearing and you will be at the disadvantage of not being able to rely upon documents. It is vital, therefore, that - although it is a small claims hearing - you should ensure you do anything you are required to do by the court.

Even if the court directions do not require the preparation and exchange of witness statements, it is a good idea to prepare statements of the oral evidence you intend to give at the hearing. By doing this, you may find favour with the Judge as he will have the opportunity to grasp the nature of the case in advance and could therefore reduce the length of the hearing. Also, by preparing a statement, you will put across all the important facts which you may not be remember to do when it comes to your turn to speak.

What I have learned from acting for clients recently, in small claims cases, is that being prepared and complying with any court directions on time is the key to succeeding. This may seem like obvious advice but it is these simple things that litigants in person can often overlook. They seem to take the view that because a claim is classified as a "small claim" then little attention needs to be paid to the presentation of the case. In a recent case, I was instructed to attend the hearing of behalf of the Defendant. Both parties had not filed at court, or served on the other side, documents and statements fourteen days before the hearing, as required by the court directions. I was instructed just seven days before the hearing and managed to take a short statement from my client. The other party, who was a litigant in person, provided their documents and statements shortly afterwards and in advance of the hearing. It gave me an idea of what the other party was going to say; this worked to our advantage as I was able to prepare questions for cross examination. When we arrived at court, we combined the documents, which each side was relying upon, into one bundle for the District Judge. Such a simple thing makes presentation much easier and the District Judge can follow the arguments much better if they have a bundle of the documents of each party to work from. Ideally, the combined bundle should be paginated.

Many litigants in person forget that they need to provide a statement of what they intend to say at the small claims hearing. Although the small claims hearing is dealt with informally, having a statement of your oral evidence will not only save valuable court time, and possibly avoid the need for an adjournment, but it will also assist you in being able to put questions to the other party. If you turn up at a small claims hearing without either party having exchanged witness statements then you will have no advance warning of what the other party is going to say. They can waffle on about any issue which might have some relevance to the case and it will be very difficult for you to put meaningful questions to your opponent. If the parties have witness statements then, before the hearing, you can look for inconsistencies in their case and question them about it at the hearing. In reality, questioning about inconsistencies in a case is the heart of cross-examination. At the hearing, if there is a statement from the party and witnesses then the Judge will ask the maker of the statement to indicate that it is their signature of the statement and whether they wish to add anything further. So the written statement - to a large degree - will form the evidence of that party/witness. You can see how having statements can save the court a considerable amount of time as the party or witness does not have to give the evidence but is merely asked questions about what is in the statement.

Although you may think that, where a party has not filed a witness statement in line with the court directions, you may want to exploit that fact at the hearing and try to prevent the other party from presenting any oral evidence; this approach may not succeed because the District Judge may allow a litigant in person some latitude and allow them to give oral evidence even though no prior statement has been exchanged. Alternatively, the District Judge might permit an adjournment subject to them paying the other party's reasonable costs and so allow documents and statements to be filed at court and exchanged. If there is an adjournment then it could take many months for the case to be relisted and, where you are the Claimant, there is the obvious delay in obtaining Judgment and being empowered to collect the money owed to you. Therefore, it might be better to try and cooperate with the other party and agree to allow documents to be relied on – provided that you do have at least a few days to consider them before the hearing. If the parties cooperate in respect of preparing a bundle, and this enables the small claims hearing to go ahead as planned, you will be saving the court time and finding favour with the Judge as you have attempted to act reasonably rather than simply win by playing procedural "games". This approach, in my opinion, is appropriate where your opponent is not represented. If your opponent has been legally represented from early in the case then you would, perhaps, be less willing to give your opponent the opportunity to exchange documents and statements later than that directed by the court.

The content of witness statements

The court requires witness statements to be set out in a particular way. As this is a small claim, the Judge will not be too concerned if a layperson makes some minor errors in the layout of the statement. However, the Judge will expect the statements to contain certain vital ingredients. A witness statement should contain the following:

- The title of the case including the case number

- The name and address of the person making the statement

- Set out in numbered paragraphs a first person narrative of the evidence which the witness will give at the hearing

- A signed statement of truth

A lawyer is will be skilled at drafting witness statements as it is part of his every day job, - especially those involved in court work. To the layperson, preparing a statement may not be such an easy task. From my experience, I have seen a tendency for laypeople to either include too much information in the witness statement or to use the statement as a vehicle to argue the merits of their case. When writing a witness statement, it is best to try and keep certain principles in mind. A witness statement should be a first person narrative of the events as the witness recalls them. It should avoid containing opinions. A good statement will stick to describing the facts as you directly experienced them. If you believe a fact to be true but did not have direct knowledge of it, then you should state the basis of your belief.

The fact that the court will direct the parties to send to the court and exchange on the other party the documents and statements they intend to rely on could mean that there are two separate bundles of documents before the court at the small claims hearing. If your opponent has legal representation (for example; you may be up against an insurer or a large organisation) it makes sense to combine the two bundles into one and to compile a single index. If you go to a small claims hearing with two badly prepared bundles with inadequate page numbering and documents being repeated in both bundles, the District Judge may become very irritated because it will be extremely difficult to locate the relevant - and important - documents. Even if you do not wish to combine the two bundles, you should, at least, clearly number your bundle and have an index at the front. You should avoid chucking every document in your possession into the bundle. Only include a document if it is necessary. Keeping a bundle down to a manageable size is important. With a small bundle of perhaps no more than 50 pages, you should focus on your best points and the crucial documents to enable you to put across your case to the District Judge in the best possible way.

SUMMARY

The key to preparing for a small claims hearing is to ensure that you follow the directions received from the court. Do not leave the preparation of statements and the bundle of documents to the last minute. Remember that even a party to the proceedings should file a statement of the evidence to be given at the small claims hearing. Try to keep statements to a manageable size and stick to a factual first person narrative of events. Be selective as to the documents that you deliver to the court, and the Defendant, as you do not want to distract the Judge's attention from the key issues by including numerous and relevant documents.

Chapter 5

The Hearing

Introduction

The hearing of a small claim is informal. It usually takes place in the District Judge's chambers. All small claims are in open court unless the Judge rules otherwise. However, there is usually limited room in chambers for spectators.

A small claims hearing is unlikely to last longer than two hours and so you will need to ensure that your case is put across in a concise manner. To do so will require good preparation. When you arrive at the court building, you should sign in with the court usher. Arrive at least 15 to 20 minutes before the scheduled start time and if your opponent has also arrived prior to the hearing then consider speaking to them to see whether or not a last-minute agreement can be reached. The court usher will usually announce when the Judge is ready to hear your case. In some courts, instead of the usher taking the parties through to the Judge's chambers, the Judge will call both parties to his chambers by announcing the case over the court "Tannoy®" system. If this is the case then it is important to listen carefully for when your case is called.

When you walk into the courtroom, the Claimant normally sits on the left hand side as you look towards the Judge. It does not matter if you fail to remember this point of etiquette. As you walk into to the courtroom remember that first impressions count enormously and you may wish to smile politely at the Judge and say either "good morning" or "good afternoon". If the District Judge is a man, when addressing him you should say 'Sir' and if the Judge is a lady then you should use the term "Ma'am". The first thing you should do when you sit down, and when the Judge does *not* initiate introduction, is to clearly introduce yourself by saying, for example, "I am Mr Fred Smith, the Claimant in this case." It is usual for the Claimant to go first and set out their case followed by the Defendant asking questions of the Claimant and his or her witnesses. The Defendant will follow and set out his or her case with the Claimant putting questions to the Defendant and any witnesses. At the end, each party will usually be given an opportunity to make a short closing statement summarising their case.

It might be that the Judge already has a good understanding of the claim from the papers and so rather than ask the parties to formally present their case, he or she might ask some relevant questions to elicit further information or clarify issues so that the Judge is able to decide the case.

The Judge does not wear a wig or gown; this adds to the informality. The strict rules of evidence do not apply and so the District Judge has the power to conduct the hearing as he/she feels is appropriate. The Judge will probably ask that any oral evidence be given under oath. If a party is not represented at the hearing then the District Judge will usually assist by asking the witnesses appropriate questions. In fact, the Judge will take a fairly active role. Even if a party is represented, it is unlikely that the advocate will be permitted to make lengthy contributions.

When you address the Judge it is advisable to speak slowly and keep an eye on the reaction you receive, as it will indicate whether or not the Judge has noted your point and/or make you aware of the necessity to further explain your argument or move on to your next point. In some respects, you can never fully prepare for a court hearing and to some extent you should not have a precise script that you wish to deliver to the Judge because, quite often, a case will drift off down an unexpected "avenue". If the Judge asks you a question then listen to it carefully and try to answer it directly; if you do not know the answer then simply say so to the Judge rather than make up some unconvincing waffle! If the Judge raises any issues against your case, and you can't seem to persuade the Judge to take your view on that point, it is probably best not to dwell on the topic and move to your next point. It may well be that your other arguments are more significant and so you do not necessarily need to worry if the Judge is not with you on one particular aspect of your case.

Experience has taught me that there will be days when the Judge appears to be wholly on your side and in such cases you will probably have to say very little at the hearing. This will probably be a case where the Judge has thoroughly read the papers and has formed a preliminary view on the case. If you are in that fortunate situation then you can sit back and let the Judge takeover - safe in the knowledge that the Judge appears to be on your side. Such a situation might arise where the defence clearly shows weaknesses and the Judge will spend most of the hearing try to ascertain from the Defendant on what basis he is disputing the claim. However, it might not be so easy to assess which way the Judge is leaning and, even up to the very last minute, Judges will want to present the appearance of having weighed up the arguments from both sides of the case before delivering their Judgment.

Preparing your case

The key to doing well at a small claims hearing is preparation. You should ensure that you have complied with all the steps you were required to do so as ordered by the court. These steps, referred to as court directions, will usually require you to send to the court and the other party all documents and signed witness statements that you intend to rely on at the hearing at least 14 days before the trial. You should ensure that you meet the deadline otherwise you will be hampered by the fact that the Judge may not allow you to rely on any documents or give any oral evidence.

To illustrate how to present your case, consider the following case study:

Case Study: Carol and Clifford

In January 2005, Carol enters into a relationship with Clifford. They do not get married, but after a courtship of 6 months, Carol moves in with Clifford. Clifford is an accountant and, at that time, his accountancy practice was going through a difficult period. He asks Carol if she could lend him £4,000 because he needed the cash to pay his daughter's school fees. Carol pays him the money in March 2007 and says that he can repay it in 12 months time. The relationship between Carol and Clifford breaks down after three years in January 2008 and Carol asks Clifford to repay what she regarded as a loan. Clifford refuses as he claims it was a gift. Carol does not pursue this debt for sometime but in January 2012 she is in financial difficulty and so Carol employs a debt collection agency called "Easy Money" to chase Clifford for the unpaid loan. In a telephone conversation between Mrs Chaser of Easy Money and Clifford, he agrees to repay the debt at £500 per month. Clifford makes a payment in February 2012 but then stops paying. Carol takes no further action until July 2012. Clifford refuses to pay and so Carol issues a claim in Upton County Court for the balance of £3,500 plus interest on 1 April 2013. Clifford disputes the claim saying that it was a loan and alleges that her claim is outside the limitation period of 6 years.

An extract of particulars of Carol's claim are set out below:

In the Upton County Court   Claim No.

Between:

Carol Smith

Claimant

And

Clifford Jones

Defendant

Particulars of claim
----

1. In March 2007, the Claimant loaned the sum of £4,000 to the Defendant. It was agreed that the Defendant could repay the loan after 12 months without the payment of interest.
2. The Claimant requested repayment of the loan in January 2008.
3. In January 2012, the Claimant employed a debt collection agency to pursue the unpaid amount. In a telephone conversation with an employee of the debt collection agency, the Defendant entered into an arrangement to repay the loan at the rate of £500 per month with the first payment to be made on 1 February 2012.
4. On 1 February 2012, the Defendant made a payment of £500.
5. The Claimant claims the sum of £3,500 plus interest pursuant to section 69 of the County Courts Act 1984 at the rate of 8% per annum from xxxxxx to the date of this claim.

Clifford enters a defence. An extract of the Defence is below:

Defence:

1. The Defendant denies that he owes the Claimant the sum claimed or any amount for the reasons set out below.
2. The Defendant admits that he received the sum of £4,000 but denies that it was a loan. The Defendant contends that it was a gift.
3. The Defendant denies paragraph 3. The Defendant admits he made a payment of £500 to the Claimant but contends that this was a gift.
4. Further and in the alternative, the Defendant contends that the Claimant's claim is statute barred under section 5 of the Limitation

Act 1980.

The key points of the defence are that Clifford says that the £4,000 was a gift and the claim is outside the limitation period for bringing a claim, which - in this - case is 6 years.

Carol has to show that, on the balance of probability, the payment of £4,000 was a loan and not a gift. The other issue is whether her claim is statute barred. Even if she did make a loan, Clifford will argue that the claim has been brought more than 6 years after March 2007. The counter argument is that, under section 29 of the Limitation Act 1980, acknowledging a debt and making part payments have the effect of renewing the limitation period from the date of acknowledgment or payment. Clifford made a payment on 1 February 2012, which would mean the limitation period would run from that date.

The case of Carol and Clifford revolves around what was said and so a statement from the parties, as to the oral evidence they will give, will assist the court.

The evidence that Carol should present to the court includes:

1. Oral evidence from herself as to the circumstances surrounding the payment of £4,000.
2. Oral evidence, from Mrs Chaser, of the telephone conversation in January 2012.
3. Letter from Mrs Chaser, sent to Clifford, confirming the conversation in January 2012.

The witness statement of Carol Smith is set out below.

IN THE UPTON COUNTY COURT   Case Number: 7UP00133

Between:

Carol Smith

Claimant

And

Clifford Jones

Defendant

Witness Statement of Carol Smith

I, Carol Smith, of 55 Market Street, Upton, will say as follows:

1. I am the Claimant in these proceedings. Except where I have indicated, this statement is from information within my own knowledge. Where it is not, I have stated the source of my belief.

2. I first met Clifford Jones in about October 2004. He was playing golf at the local country club and I was working behind the bar. In about January 2005, I moved in with him. Clifford is an accountant but I recall that at that time he was experiencing financial difficulties with his practice. He has a daughter, Rebecca, by his first marriage and at that time she was at Upton Manor School for girls, which is a fee-paying private school. I recall, around March 2007, we discussed the fact that the school had been pressing for overdue school fees and, unless they were paid, Rebecca would be asked to leave. Clifford was very concerned about this and he asked whether I could lend him £4,000 to cover the school fees. I was happy to lend him the money and said that he did not have to pay it back for 12 months; nor did he need to pay interest. I remember having this conversation about the school fees and the loan because we had gone away to Barbados for a fortnight and I remember he kept saying he was extremely grateful, whereas I kept saying he did not need to be as we had a stable relationship and I believed we had a future together.

3. In about January 2008, our relationship started to breakdown and I recall that I asked Clifford to repay the money. His first response was that he would let me have the money by the end of the month. When the end of the month arrived and he had not repaid the loan, I spoke to him on the telephone and he said that the £4,000 was a gift and would not be paying me any money.

4. I did not chase Clifford for the money for sometime, apart from the occasional telephone conversation on his mobile. I did not write to him as he did not say where he was living. I suppose that I did not chase him much for the money as I felt that, although we had split up, I thought he was a decent person and would pay me when he

was able to. However, by the end of 2011, my finances were quite tight and I decided that I had given Clifford long enough and so I instructed a debt recovery agency called "Easy Money".

5. In January 2012, Easy Money told me that they had spoken to Clifford and he had agreed to repay the loan at £500 per month with the first payment to be received on the 1 February 2012 and each month thereafter. On the 1 February 2012, I received £500 from Clifford but I have not received any further payments since then.

STATEMENT OF TRUTH

I believe that the facts in this witness statement are true

Signed Carol Smith   Date   1 November xxxx
          Claimant

The other important piece of evidence to support Carol's claim is the oral evidence of Mrs Chaser at Easy Money. Carol should ask her to make a statement in the same format.   An extract of her statement is set out below:

1. *I was instructed by Carol Smith to chase a Clifford Jones in respect of an unpaid loan of £4,000. I spoke to Mr Jones on 20 January 2012 at 2pm. He had called the office in response to my letter on 15 January 2012 demanding payment within 7 days otherwise we would take legal action.*
2. *Mr Jones said that he realised he owed money to Carol Smith but due to financial difficulties, he wanted to pay by instalments. He offered to pay £500 per month with the first payment to be made on 1 February 2012. I spoke to Carol Smith and she agreed to accept this offer. I then wrote a letter to Clifford Smith confirming the arrangement.*

When Carol receives Clifford's statement she can start preparing her line of questioning for the hearing. An extract from Clifford's witness statement is set out below:

I met Carol Smith in October 2004. By January 2005, she had moved in with me. I recall at the time that my accountancy practice was not doing as well as it had been and so I had to tighten my belt. I mentioned this to Carol in the spring of 2007 and I said that we probably could not afford to go on holiday for a fortnight to a luxury hotel in Barbados that we had planned because I was just managing to cover my daughter's school fees. Carol said that she was willing to pay for the holiday and she said to me, "Book the holiday on your credit card and I will give you a cheque for £4,000 when the card bill comes in at the end of the month." The money was not a loan but a gift. Carol had not said that I had to repay the money when she gave it to me.

At the end of 2011, I was surprised to receive letters from a debt collection agency "Easy Money". I was aware through a mutual friend that Carol was having a difficult time financially and so I felt sorry for her and sent a cheque to her for £500. This was not made as a payment of any loan; it was a gift.

The hearing of Carol's claim has been allocated 90 minutes. This should be ample time as the average length of a small claims hearing is approximately 1 hour.

If you are required to formally put your case in a structured way it would be advisable to prepare an outline of what you want to say ensuring that all the main points are covered. You will probably be quite nervous about speaking in court. All of your comments should be addressed to the Judge. If your opponent interrupts and starts throwing insults at you when you are talking, resist the temptation to respond and engage in an argument; leave it to the Judge to intervene. By staying calm and avoiding a "tit for tat" shouting match, you are more likely to find favour with the Judge.

Do you need legal representation at the hearing?

A small claims hearing can be conducted in any manner that the District Judge thinks fit. In some instances, the Judge may conduct the hearing in a formal manner or it might be more informal and simply ask each party questions about their case. Sometimes the case may involve legal argument and on those occasions it may assist to have a lawyer present to represent you. Of course, it could be argued that if the points of law are very complex then it may be that the case should be allocated to the Fast Track where the stricter rules of evidence apply and legal costs can be awarded and so make it more viable for lawyers to present the arguments to the Judge. Legal representation is not essential at a small claims hearing; if you feel confident and able to present your case in a clear and concise way then you should be able to cope with representing yourself.

There other occasions where having a lawyer at the hearing could be an advantage. A particular case is where there is antagonism between the parties and, although the District Judge will obviously attempt to control the situation, having a lawyer present in such situations can help maintain order. The lawyer will help avoid you falling in to the trap of having a verbal slanging match in the court. If there has been animosity between you and the other side then it may be difficult for you put questions to the other party. I have seen on many occasions how litigants in person experience difficulty in framing actual questions to the other party or a witness. What tends to happen is that questions come out as statements instead of actual questions initially designed to expose a weakness in the other's case.

The following dialogue is an example of what might be said at the hearing of "**Carol Smith v. Clifford Jones**":

Carol:
"Sir, my claim is for the sum of £3,500 which is the balance of the amount I loaned to Mr Jones in March 2007. I trust that you have read my statement that I filed at court?
District Judge:
I have glanced at the statement before the hearing but please take me through the main points.
Carol:
As you can see, in March 2007 we had discussed the fact that Mr Jones was going through financial difficulties and was finding it hard to pay for his daughter's school fees. I said that I would be happy to lend him the money and he could pay me back in 12 months time without interest. It was not until our relationship came to an end in January 2008 that I asked for the repayment of the loan. He said that he would repay me at the end of the month, which he did not. I later instructed Easy Money debt collection agency to pursue him and, as you can see from the statement of Mrs Chaser, he agreed in January 2012 to repay me at £500 per month and, indeed, he made a payment in February 2012 but nothing further.
District Judge:
Thank you Ms Smith. Mr Jones, I see that you do not deny receiving the £4,000 but say that it was a loan?
Clifford:

That is correct Sir. I was finding my finances a little tight at the time and Carol wanted to go on holiday to Barbados. She told me to book the holiday on my credit card and she would pay the card bill when it came in. There was nothing mentioned that it was a loan.

District Judge*:*
Mr Jones, but can you explain why you made a payment of £500 following a conversation you had with Mrs Chaser of Easy Money?
Clifford:
I made the payment of £500 as I had heard thorough a mutual friend that Carol was having financial difficulties and I felt sympathy for her and so sent the money. I dispute that I said to Mr Chaser that I owed £4,000 to Carol or that I would pay £500 per month.
District Judge:
Then why did Mrs Chaser write a letter to you confirming the conversation?
Clifford:
I have never received such a letter.
District Judge:
Ms Smith, would you like to ask Mr Jones any questions?
Carol:
Yes, I would. Clifford, why did you pay me £500 in February 2012 if, as you allege, you never made any agreement with Mrs Chaser of Easy Money?
Clifford:
I heard through a mutual acquaintance that you were having money problems and I thought you could do with the money.
Carol:
Who was this "mutual acquaintance"?
Clifford:
I don't recall his name.
District Judge:
Mr Jones, do you wish to ask Ms Smith any questions?
Clifford:
No sir.
District Judge:
In which case, I will now give my Judgment.

Under Practice Direction 27, the Judge may give reasons for his Judgment as briefly and as simply as the nature of the case allows. He will normally do so at the end of hearing but he may give them later at a later date either orally or in writing.

In the case of Carol Smith v Clifford Jones, it is likely that the Judge would give his decision straightaway. In view of the evidence presented by both parties, it is likely that the District Judge would find as follows:

"This is a claim by Ms Carol Smith for the sum of £3,500 which she asserts is the balance due on a loan she made to Mr Clifford Jones in March 2007. Mr Jones in his Defence has claimed that the money was a gift. I am satisfied on the balance of probability that Ms Smith loaned Mr Jones the money. Mr Jones has further argued that the claim by Ms Smith was brought outside the limitation period. Ms Smith has presented the evidence of Mrs Chaser from Easy Money that Mr Jones entered into an agreement to repay the loan at £500 per month and in February 2012; she received £500. I am satisfied on the balance of probability that the payment of £500 made by Mr Jones was not a gift but was in fact the first instalment in respect of the agreement he reached with Mrs Chaser of Easy Money. Therefore, the payment of £500 in February was an acknowledgment of the debt and I find that the limitation period started to run from February 2012 and so the claim by Ms Smith is not outside the limitation period. I therefore grant Judgment for Claimant in the sum of £3,500 plus court fees and interest. Ms Smith, what is the amount of interest? [Ms Smith gives the Judge the figure].The Judgment is to be paid within 14 days."

Summary

The District Judge may conduct a small claims hearing in any way he/she thinks is appropriate. You do not need to have a legal representative with you at the hearing but it might be advisable to consider having one if the case contains issues of law that might well be better explained to the Judge by someone who is legally qualified. You may also wish to consider a legal representative at the hearing if you do not feel confident enough to present your case at the court. The hearing is informal and usually held in a Judge's chambers, but some individuals will feel that the hearing is too much of an ordeal to handle by themselves without a legal representative being present.

Chapter 6

Costs in the small claims track

Introduction

It is probably well known that, in the Small Claims Track, cases are subject to the general rule that legal fees will not be awarded; only court fees and certain fixed costs can be recovered, as stated in CPR Part 27. This is the reason why the majority of Small Claims are conducted by litigants in person. As was indicated in a previous chapter, it is sensible to spend some money on legal advice as to the merits of a claim and receive guidance as to how to set out your case. However, the general rule about legal costs is why many Claimants will skip taking proper legal advice and in some cases will resort to obtaining advice by posting on internet forums. What they receive is, typically, unqualified guidance, which will sometimes totally miss the point or ramble on about irrelevant issues. The old adage of "a little knowledge is dangerous" certainly applies here. For the reason of limited fixed costs, it is understandable that people will be reluctant to seek legal advice. What is less well known is the set of circumstances wherein it may be possible to recover some legal fees from the losing party.

What the court rules say about legal fees in small claims

The Civil Procedure Rules (CPR) state, at Part 27.14(2), the position as to costs:

(2) The court may not order a party to pay a sum to another party in respect of that other party's costs, fees and expenses, including those relating to an appeal, except –

(a) the fixed costs attributable to issuing the claim which –

(i) are payable under Part 45; or

(ii) would be payable under Part 45 if that Part applied to the claim;

(b) in proceedings which included a claim for an injunction or an order for specific performance a sum not exceeding the amount specified in Practice Direction 27 for legal advice and assistance relating to that claim;

(c) any court fees paid by that other party;

(d) expenses which a party or witness has reasonably incurred in travelling to and from a hearing or in staying away from home for the purposes of attending a hearing;

(e) a sum not exceeding the amount specified in Practice Direction 27 for any loss of earnings or loss of leave by a party or witness due to attending a hearing or to staying away from home for the purposes of attending a hearing;

(f) a sum not exceeding the amount specified in Practice Direction 27 for an expert's fees;

(g) such further costs as the court may assess by the summary procedure and order to be paid by a party who has behaved unreasonably

So in addition to being able to recover the court fees, the sum permitted for seeking advice in relation to an injunction or an order for specific performance is £260. The figure for witness expenses is a sum not exceeding £90 per day. If the Claim Form was issued by a solicitor then a small fixed sum for "legal representative's costs" can be added to the claim amount. These vary depending on the size of the claim:

Amount of the Claim	Level of fixed solicitors costs added to Claim amount on Issue
Value of claim exceeds £25 but does not exceed £500	£50
Value of claim exceeds £500 but does not exceed £1000	£70
Value of claim exceeds £1000 but does not exceed £5,000	£80
The claim exceeds £5000	£100

It is important to remember that the above fixed costs can only be added where a solicitor is acting and issues the Claim Form.

So, apart from the court fees, fixed solicitors' costs on issue, limited witness expenses and expert fees, the only other situation where the rules permit legal fees to be recovered is under CPR Part 27.14(2)(g) where a party has behaved unreasonably. Some examples that have been found to be unreasonable behaviour include:

- failing to turn up for the final hearing without notifying the court in advance that you will not be attending and inviting the court to take into account the documents and statements you have submitted;

- pulling out of a case at the last minute when there has been no change in the circumstances;

- the pursuit of a case which is both unsupported by evidence and speculative;

- pressing a case which is essentially hopeless with an ulterior motive of embarrassing or inconveniencing the opposite party;

- causing adjournments by not turning up at a hearing without a reasonable excuse;

- making a dishonest claim;

- ignoring a reasonable offer to settle in advance of the hearing;

A party's rejection of an offer in settlement will not, by itself, constitute unreasonable behaviour under paragraph (2)(g) but the court may take it into consideration when applying the unreasonableness test.

Successfully arguing that there has been unreasonable conduct is not as easy as it might seem. The first problem is that the CPR provides no express definition of what constitutes a party's unreasonable behaviour. Also, the limited case law on the subject is very case-specific and is difficult to extract any clear principles. After you have won a case, you are quite likely to say it was obvious from the beginning that you were going to succeed or the rejection of the offer was unreasonable, but in these circumstances your view of "unreasonable conduct" is not objective.

The reality is that District Judges rarely make orders for costs in small claims based on unreasonable conduct unless there is something fairly exceptional in the case and so can be regarded as a waste of the other party's and court's time. However, parties to small claim should be aware of the way they conduct proceedings as there is risk of being subject to a costs order.

Can I claim legal costs under a contractual term in the contract?

There have been attempts to argue that if a contract contains a provision for the award of legal costs then - despite the case being subject to the provisions of the small claims track - legal fees should be awarded. There have been a number of cases recently on this subject. The case of **Robert Shaw v Nine Regions Limited (2009)** took the view that a party was entitled to costs under a contractual provision even though the claim was in the small claims track. However, in the case **Graham v Sand Martin Heights Residents Company Limited (2011)**, HHJ Maloney QC decided that, in a case allocated to the small claims track, there is no basis to award the winning party his costs of legal representation unless there was unreasonable behaviour under CPR Part 27.14(2)(g). He said that this was not affected by a provision in a contract for legal costs.

The decision, in **Shaw**, was arrived at in the High Court, whereas, in **Graham**, it was in the *County* Court. HHJ Maloney QC referred to this in his Judgment and said that it would have been binding on him unless it had been decided *"per incuriam"* which means it was wrongly decided because he did not have regard to authority, which was binding on the Judge and would have led him to a different conclusion. So HHJ Maloney QC took the view that the Judge in **Shaw** had not considered the authority of the provisions in CPR Part 27. Had he done so, he would have not come to the conclusion that there was entitlement to costs under the contract.

"Reasonable collection costs" under the Late Payment of Commercial Debts Regulations 2013

It has already been mentioned that, where there is a commercial debt, there is an entitlement, under the Late Payment of Commercial Debts Regulations 2013, to claim reasonable collection costs. Reasonable collection costs can include legal fees as the European Directive (which the Regulations implement) states, at Article 6, that reasonable collection costs includes the expenses of instructing a lawyer. This would seem to be at odds with CPR Part 27, but as European Law is supreme we can say these regulations override CPR Part 27. However, I was involved in a recent small claim where there was an entitlement to receive legal fees, under the Late Payment of Commercial Debts Regulations, as reasonable collection costs; however, the District Judge did not award legal fees. The reality is that, although there may be entitlement to legal fees under the Regulations, some District Judges may still not award costs and the amount in question, with regard to legal fees, would probably not make it worthwhile pursuing an appeal.

SUMMARY

The general position, in relation to costs in a small claim, is that, on winning your case, you will only be awarded the court fee and certain fixed costs. In some limited situations, legal fees may be awarded by the District Judge, for example where the other party has clearly acted unreasonably in their conduct of the case. In a situation of a business chasing a commercial debt, and the provisions of the Late Payment of Commercial Debts Regulations apply, it is possible – though not guaranteed - to recover reasonable collection costs, and these can include lawyer's fees.

Chapter 7

How to appeal a small claims decision

If you go to a small claims hearing, and the Judgment does not go in your favour, you might have grounds to present an appeal. The word "might" cannot be emphasized enough. The court rules - and the relevant case law - set out the grounds for an appeal. Even if you can establish grounds for persuading a Circuit Judge to overturn the decision of the District Judge, it will involve careful legal argument and is something the layperson might not be able to handle on their own. Add to this fact that legal costs are no longer available in a small claims appeal; it makes it very difficult to successfully appeal a small claims decision.

If you are unhappy with the decision then it is vital that you get proper legal advice promptly. You have a limited period of 21 days in which to lodge the appeal. Appeals are almost always on points of law and not on issues of fact unless the conclusion reached by the Judge was deemed evidently illogical. If the District Judge considered all the facts that he should have considered then the only realistic chance of an appeal is if the Judge's decision was an error of law. The reason why appeal courts will not usually interfere with a finding of fact is that the appeal courts take the view that the Judge who heard the evidence at the trial was best placed to make decisions as to the credibility of witnesses and to apply appropriate weight to the evidence.

At the end of the hearing you can ask the Judge for permission to appeal. You will be required to say on what basis you are asking the District Judge to grant permission to appeal. The Judge will either grant or refuse permission to appeal. If permission to appeal is refused, which is the case in the vast majority of claims, you have to seek permission in the application that you lodge at the court. If that is the case then the Circuit Judge who hears appeals from small claims matters will first have to consider if permission to appeal should be granted and then – in the event permission *is* granted - go on to consider the appeal.

If you are to obtain permission to appeal you will have to convince the court that there is a real prospect of success or that there is some other compelling reason why the appeal should be heard. A real prospect of success means that the prospect of success must be realistic rather than fanciful. Any failure, by original the District Judge, to address an issue may be regarded as a compelling reason why an appeal should be heard. Where the Circuit Judge refuses permission to appeal, the person seeking permission may ask for the decision to be reconsidered at an oral hearing.

Starting an appeal does not have the effect of staying a Judgment. Therefore, you need to apply in the appeal notice to stay the Judgment; otherwise, the other party can proceed to enforce the order if they were awarded a sum of money or costs.

Assuming permission to appeal is granted, the Circuit Judge will go on to consider the grounds of appeal. The grounds for allowing appeals are that the decision of the lower court was wrong or it was unjust because of a serious procedural, or other, irregularity in the proceedings in the lower court. In addition, a decision will only be wrong if the matter of complaint would have made a difference to the decision of the lower court.

It is important to examine what is meant by *"the decision of the lower court was wrong"*. It is not just a matter of you thinking the Judge should have made a different decision! "Wrong" means unsustainable. If there is a technical error then it will not mean the decision was wrong if it was based on an insubstantial point. So, when you consider the other evidence, it may mean that - despite the error - the lower court's decision was not wrong.

The procedure for making an appeal is to file form N164. You will be required to attach a copy of the order being appealed. If you are going to appeal you should obtain a transcript of the Judgment as soon as possible. There are a number of companies that deal with transcribing court Judgments. The cost of getting a transcript is not usually excessive. If you are not able to enclose a copy of the Judgment with form N164 then you should state that the transcript will follow. Do not miss the deadline for filing the appeal.

Upon receiving the appeal, and the required court fee, the County Court office will refer the notice to the Circuit Judge for that area who deals with appeals. The Circuit Judge will consider the application and if permission to appeal has not been granted then that will be the first matter for consideration. If permission to appeal is granted then the Circuit Judge will usually issue directions which will normally include filing a copy of the Judgment transcript within a period of time and also requiring the appellant (the person making the appeal) to prepare a bundle of documents for the appeal hearing. The appellant will be required to send copies to the respondent. The court will list the appeal for a date with a time estimate, which will probably be in the region of 90 minutes. The court directions for the appeal may also require the filing of skeleton arguments prior to the hearing of the appeal. A skeleton argument is a summary of the legal points that you intend to make at the court hearing.

Summary

If you think there is a basis to appeal the small claims decision then you should ask for permission to appeal and at the end of the hearing. It is likely to be refused and you will need to seek permission on the appeal form N164; this must be filed at court within 21 days of the small claims hearing.

Chapter 8

Enforcing a Judgment

Once you have obtained Judgment, you might think you can put your feet up and wait for the court to send you your money; you couldn't be more wrong! For a start, the court does not enforce (collect your money); you have to instruct it to follow a procedure and this will incur further court fees. This may come as a surprise, as many might think that a Judgment of the court is all you need to make the Defendant hand over their money. It may also be surprising to discover that the percentage of unsatisfied small claims Judgments (those remaining unpaid) is very high; around a quarter of small claims Judgments obtained during 2011 remained unsatisfied.

The Tribunal Courts & Enforcement Act 2007 was hailed as "the cure" for all enforcement problems in the civil justice system. Many of the provisions of this Act remain unimplemented with some having just been introduced. Some of the new measures may not help the creditor in recovering unpaid Judgments, such as the requirement for enforcement agents (bailiffs) to give 7 days notice before attending to try and take control of goods. Whilst the intention was to regulate and improve bailiffs, the consequence of introducing greater protection against abuse by some rogue bailiffs has caused (in the opinion of creditors) a system that appears to "bend over backwards" to help debtors avoid paying their debts.

Despite a system that is, seemingly, heavily weighted in favour of the Judgment debtor, we ought to remain positive and consider that the best way to enforce Judgments is to be armed with lots of relevant information about the circumstances of the debtor to enable you to select the best enforcement process.

If you have evidence to suggest that a debtor will move assets/sell property to avoid enforcement then - at the end of the small claims hearing - you could ask the District Judge to grant an injunction under CPR Part 25.1(1) (f) which states that a court may grant:

(f) an order (referred to as a 'freezing injunction) –
(i) restraining a party from removing from the jurisdiction assets located there; or
(ii) restraining a party from dealing with any assets whether located within the jurisdiction or not;

The Order is an interim order and so it could be used to aid enforcement in the same way as the County Court Remedies Regulations 1991 (SI 1991/1222) could be used to ask for an injunction to aid enforcement of a Judgment. These 1991 Regulations were revoked in April 2014. An injunction under CPR Part 25.1(1)(f) may be granted - for a limited period - to enable you, for example, to apply and obtain a charging order over the Defendant's property if there was evidence that, before the application could be considered, the Defendant may attempt to dispose of the property.

What are the methods of enforcement?

- High Court Enforcement Officers/County Court bailiffs
- Third party debt orders
- Attachment of earnings orders
- Charging orders, followed by Orders for Sale
- Bankruptcy
- Winding up petitions
- Order to Attend Court for Questioning

Strictly speaking, not all of the above are methods of enforcement. For example, an Order to Attend Court for Questioning is a method by which the creditor can obtain more information about the finances of the debtor so that the creditor can select the most appropriate method of enforcement.

County Court Bailiff/High Court Enforcement Officers

The most common form of enforcement is that of a bailiff, either in the form a County Court bailiff or High Court enforcement officer (HCEO). This is probably because it has become part of legal folklore that, when you want to collect/realise the sum due under an unpaid Judgment, you "send in the bailiffs". It may be the most widely known, but it may not always be the most effective method. Perhaps the lack of effectiveness may be connected with a greater awareness by debtors of the limits on what bailiffs can do.

There are limits on what they can do but you may not want to spend large amounts on trying to achieve payment of the Judgment debt. For example, if you decide to instruct a high court enforcement officer then the cost of doing so and the liability for future costs - if the officer is not successful - is relatively low. At the time writing, if you have a Judgment debt of more than £600 then, for a court fee of £60, you can transfer the Judgment up to the High Court for enforcement by a High Court Enforcement Agent. If they are successful in obtaining payment of the debt from the debtor then the High Court Enforcement Agent will recover their costs from the debtor. If they are not successful then there will be a small abortive fee – currently, £75 plus VAT.

Provisions in the Tribunal Courts and Enforcement Act 2007 were finally introduced, during April 2014, which brought in changes to bailiff law and the associated terminology. Bailiffs and High Court Enforcement Officers are now referred to as "Enforcement Agents". Much of the change in terminology concerns re-naming the "seizing of goods" to "taking control of goods". Also, High Court Enforcement Agents have to give at least 7 days notice to the Judgment debtor, before attending, to execute a warrant. This aspect of the new provisions is, obviously, not helpful to a creditor; however, when I spoke with with high court enforcement companies - after the implementation - they did not feel it would have a huge impact on their effectiveness. It is probably not going to affect their recovery rates where they are attending premises that are open to the public, such as pubs and restaurants, or where the Judgment debtor is not going to be able to move goods within that 7-day notice period. The other important change is that there will now be set fees for High Court Enforcement Agents. The set fees are considerably lower than the previous fee scale and, in reality, some High Court Enforcement companies are going to find it difficult to survive. Indeed, some companies are diversifying into other areas of work.

Instructing a County Court Enforcement Agent (Bailiff)

A County Court bailiff can be instructed to attempt to take control of goods where the Judgment debt does not exceed £5,000. This is done by completing form N323 (Request for a Warrant of Control) and sending it to the County Court, where the Judgment was entered, together with the required court fee.

Transferring a County Court up to the High Court for enforcement by a High Court Enforcement Agent

Transferring County Court Judgments up to the High Court for Enforcement by a High Court Enforcement Agent does not transform the Judgment into a High Court Judgment. The Judgment is merely transferred up for the purpose of enforcement. Where the Judgment debt exceeds £600, it can be transferred up to the High Court. The advantages of enforcing through the High Court is that the Enforcement Agents usually have more incentive to collect as they are not paid civil servants, as are County Court bailiffs. The process to transfer up is straightforward. All you need to do find a High Court Enforcement company, complete certain information about the name and address of the Judgment Creditor & Judgment Debtor, and then send them a copy of the Judgment along with the court fee of £60.

An Attachment of Earnings Order

An Attachment of Earnings Order is a method by which money will be taken from the Judgment debtor's wages by their employer, who then forwards the money to the court to pass on to the Judgment creditor. This method of enforcement cannot be used where the debtor is not employed, i.e. is self-employed.

The procedure for applying for an attachment of earning order is:

a) Complete Form N337 (Request for an Attachment of Earnings Order)
b) Send the Completed form to the court, local to where the debtor resides, along with the court fee.

You send the application to the court, local to where the Defendant resides, as the County Court Money Claims Centre or Money Claim Online will not deal with the application.

The Court will send a request to the Judgment Debtor to provide details of his/her earnings. Once the court has received details of the debtor's earnings, and if there is income above the "protected rate", it will set a figure to be deducted monthly from the employee's salary. The "protected rate" is the level below which the court considers that the Judgment debtor's earnings should not be reduced.

Third party debt orders

A third-party debt order is where the Judgment creditor can obtain an order compelling a third party - who owns money to the Judgment debtor - to make payment of the money directly to the creditor. A common situation when a creditor will apply for a third-party debt order is where the debtor has a bank account and the creditor will seek an order for the bank to pay any credit in the debtor's account directly to the creditor.

If you are aware of a third party who owes money to the debtor, and you have evidence to establish that is the case, then a third party debt order can be an effective means of collecting money due on a Judgment. The use of a third party debt order does come with its difficulties. For example, it may be difficult to establish that a customer owes money, or, the third party argues that the money is not owed to the Judgment debtor. The other problem, especially where you are seeking a third party debt order over the debtor's bank account, is that the order is only effective on the day it is served on the bank. So you may serve the order on Monday when there is little or no credit in the account, but two days later the debtor has a large credit balance. There are proposals to amend the rules in relation to third party debt orders so that the order can be a re-occurring attachment to the monies owed by the third party.

Although a third party debt order has its imperfections, in some situations you may be able to recover a fair amount of the Judgment owed to you. Also, as a result of the bank placing a freeze on the account in consideration of the amount due to the creditor, this inconvenience to the debtor will often make them come forward and resolve the issue of payment so that the bank account can become functional again.

To apply for a third party debt order you will need to complete form N349 and send it to the County Court, which covers the area where the Judgment debtor lives, together with the court fee. The administrative centre at Salford will send details of the case to the local County Court hearing centre so that it can process the application.

Form N349 is relatively straightforward to complete but there are a couple of points to consider when filling in the form. If you do not know the bank account number but have the sort code of the bank then the bank is required to search through all accounts in the name of the debtor. It may well be that the bank account is not – precisely – in the same name as the debtor and the bank may not bring up this account during their search. The other aspect of form N349, which you need to ensure you answer, is the basis of your belief that the third party owes the money to the debtor. In the case of a bank account, you can state that you believe it is bank account of the debtor because you have received cheques from them in the past. You might wish to exhibit to the application a copy of the evidence to support the identity of the third party.

If the court is satisfied that the application has been completed correctly, and there appears to be a basis on which the third party owes money to the creditor, then the District Judge will make an interim order. The court will then send the interim order to the third party and then - seven days later - send the order to the debtor. You may wish to say to the court, when you submit your application, that *you* will serve the interim order. You might want to do this so that you have control over when the interim order is served. If the interim order is served by you, and not the court, then you can decide when the debtor's bank account is likely to have most credit in it. The reason for serving interim orders on the third party before being served on the debtor is to ensure that the debtor is not given an opportunity to remove funds, which may be in a bank account, or contact the third party to pay him instead before the order is obtained. If you wish to serve the interim third party debt order then make it very clear when you submit the application to the court.

Charging Orders

A charging order is, strictly speaking, a means of securing a debt rather than a method of enforcement. The enforcement comes later when either the property is sold voluntarily or by an application to force a sale. You are able to apply for a charging order even if the Judgment debtor is keeping to an instalment arrangement; this rule applies to Judgments entered after 1 October 2012.

To apply for a charging order it is necessary to:

- Complete form N379 (if the charge is to be against land, otherwise complete N380)
- Pay a court fee

The form requires the following information:

- Details of the Judgment: when it was entered, at what court and under what claim number.
- The full name and address of the Judgment debtor.
- The amount of the Judgment and that which is due at the time of application.
- The address of the property or land on which you want to impose a charge.
- Information as to whether the Judgment debtor owns the property solely, or jointly with someone else, and evidence to prove it.
- Details of any other creditors you know the Judgment debtor has, with their names and addresses, and the nature of their debt.
- Details of any other person who has an interest in the property.
- Details of any additional information, apart from the fact that you are owed the money, that you want the court to consider when deciding the application.

The application contains a statement of truth and it has to be signed to confirm that the facts stated are true. If the land is registered, attach the official copy of the land register to prove that the debtor has an interest in the land. Most land in England and Wales is now registered. There are only a few old properties that remain unregistered. Every transaction involving unregistered land will automatically result in the land being registered. Proving the debtor's interest in unregistered land can be more difficult. It would be sensible to attach a witness statement to the charging order application to show the grounds for believing that the debtor has an interest in the unregistered property.

A District Judge will consider the application and, once satisfied that the debtor has an interest in the property, an interim charging order will be made with a hearing date set to consider whether the order should be made final.

The creditor will receive the interim order from the court with sufficient copies to serve on the Judgment debtor and any other parties which the court may direct. The interim order and the application must be served, not less than 21 days before the date of the hearing, on the Judgment debtor and any other person that the court directs. Before you serve the interim order on the debtor, you should register it at the Land Registry so that any person dealing with the land will have notice of the interim charging order and so the property cannot be transacted without the charge being released or, at least, being giving notice of the transaction. This is done by completing the appropriate form and sending it to the Land Registry together with the interim charging order received from the court. The form can be obtained from the Land Registry website. There is a fee but this expense is typically awarded by the court when making a final charging order. The Land Registry should be notified if the charging order is dismissed.

Orders for Sale

An order for sale is a way to realise your money after you have secured a charge over the debtor's property. The application is a new claim to the court; this is initiated by completing a Claim on Form N208. Claim Forms in the form of N208 are used where the "Part 8" procedure, of the court rules, is followed. Usually the "Part 8" procedure is used in certain types of claims, such as injunctions. Normally, where you are making a claim for money, the "Part 7" procedure is used.

Before applying for an Order for Sale, you should consider whether there will be sufficient equity in the property remaining after it is sold. If you are applying for an Order for Sale where the property charged is owned by one person/organisation then the application is governed by Part 73 of the CPR. There is certain information that should be included in the Claim Form, and this must:

(1) identify the charging order and the property sought to be sold;
(2) state the amount in respect of which the charge was imposed and the amount due at the date of issue of the claim;
(3) verify, so far as known, the debtor's title to the property charged;
(4) state, so far as the Claimant is able to identify –
   (a) the names and addresses of any other creditors who have a prior charge or other security over the property; and
   (b) the amount owed to each such creditor; and
(5) give an estimate of the price which would be obtained on sale of the property.
(6) if the claim relates to land, give details of every person who to the best of the Claimant's knowledge is in possession of the property; and
(7) if the claim relates to residential property –
(a) state whether –
   (i) a land charge of Class F; or
   (ii) a notice under section 31(10) of the Family Law Act 1996, or under any provision of an Act which preceded that section,

There are some practical difficulties in obtaining the amount that might be owed to other creditors, such as where there is a mortgage over the property. It is likely that the mortgage company is going to say it cannot give you the information because of data protection despite the fact that the CPR requires the creditor to take reasonable steps to attempt to obtain the information. Obtaining the estimated value of the property is not as difficult because there are various websites that you can search to obtain the recent sale values of properties.

If the Claim for an Order for Sale is in respect of property jointly owned, the application is made under the Trusts of Land and Appointment of Trustees Act 1996 (known by the abbreviation "TOLATA 1996"). Where you are seeking an Order for Sale of property that is jointly owned, remember to have both owners named on the Claim Form.

There is a restriction on the level of a charge below which an Order for Sale will not be made. The current figure is £1,000. There was much expectation that this figure was going to be higher, such as £25,000. The reality is that the smaller the debt, the less likely it will be for the court to grant an Order for Sale. In most cases, a District Judge will probably grant a suspended order which means that an Order will not be enforced provided certain conditions are complied with, such as keeping to an instalment arrangement. The court is likely to take into account a number of factors - such as who occupies the property - when considering whether to make an Order and when considering an application under TOLATA; the purpose for which the property was bought is also an important factor. So if the property was purchased as a family home and children are living there, it is more likely the Judge will suspend the Order. It is unlikely that a Judge will grant an outright Order on the first application if the debt is quite small and the debtor is making an effort to pay. So do not be surprised that, when you have applied for an Order for Sale, the Judge might be reluctant to grant an Order at the first hearing without suspending its enforcement on specified terms.

Bankruptcy and Winding Up

Bankruptcy is where an individual is unable to pay their debts. A bankruptcy petition can be presented against an individual if a creditor - who is owed more than £750 - serves a 'statutory demand' for the money due and it is not paid or secured (or a settlement is not agreed) within 21 days, and the debtor has not applied for the statutory demand to be set aside because of a substantial dispute about the debt being due. The last aspect as to there being no dispute is important; in reality, if there is a real dispute as to the debt being due, then you should issue a claim and get a Judgment first.

You can wind up a company and put it into liquidation if it owes you (or more than one creditor) more than £750 and you can show that the company can't pay what it owes. Section 122 of the Insolvency Act 1986 sets out when a company is regarded as not being able to pay its debts. You can bring a petition to wind up a company without actually having served a statutory demand; under Section 122, a company can be regarded as being insolvent if it cannot pay its debts as they fall due. So you can present a petition for the winding up of a company if it has failed to settle an outstanding debt, which is undisputed and is greater than £750. However, it is advisable to serve a statutory demand *before* proceeding to wind up a company because a company that has not paid a debt may not necessarily be "unable to pay its debts as they fall due".

If a person is made bankrupt, a trustee in bankruptcy (usually the Official Receiver) is appointed to realise the assets of the bankrupt and make the appropriate distributions to unsecured creditors. When a company is wound up, a liquidator is appointed to realise in the assets of the company and make any distributions to unsecured creditors. The reality is that there is often no distribution to creditors and only the Official Receiver or liquidator gets paid.

I have deliberately not said much about bankruptcy and the winding up of insolvent companies. There are a few reasons for this. Bankruptcy and insolvency is not really a method of enforcement. Also, it may sound obvious, but if a person or company is insolvent, then the reality is that there is not going to be money to pay you. There will be some cases where a company or individual will react and make payment to prevent liquidation or bankruptcy; this may include individuals who are professionals and would not be able to practice their profession (or experience extreme difficulty continuing) if they were made bankrupt. Similarly, a company that is established and wants to continue trading will probably react and make payment when faced with the prospect of being wound up. However, these situations will only be where the individuals and organisations actually have the money. So the threat of insolvency is only likely to work on those who actually have the money or have a particular reason to avoid insolvency.

Not only is there the prospect that bankruptcy or winding up will not achieve a recovery, but the costs of presenting a petition is now quite expensive. A further reason why bankruptcy or winding up may not be the answer is because, if you obtain a bankruptcy order and there were no assets to distribute, then the bankrupt person cannot be chased anymore for the debts that are included in the bankruptcy. So it has the result of wiping off debts incurred before the bankruptcy. If you were to obtain a Judgment and not seek to bankrupt an individual, you could sit back and wait for a time when the individual has more assets for you to attack.

Order to Attend Court for Questioning

If you do not have sufficient information about the debtor to make a decision as to how to enforce your Judgment, then you might consider applying for an Order to Attend Court for Questioning. This is where the debtor is required to attend court and answer questions before a court official about their finances. In my experience, this exercise is not always as useful as it may sound. The difficulties include the fact that you have to personally serve the debtor with the notice to attend court and that may not be so easy. If you do not have legal representation then you can request the court bailiff to serve the order but the reality is that court bailiffs are overstretched and may not have the time to attend on several occasions or attend at the right time to find the debtor at home.

However, there will be occasions when an Order to Attend can be a good opportunity to discover more information about the debtor's finances. To maximise the prospects of extracting useful information it is important to draft pertinent questions and request the debtor to bring to court particular documents. The form used to apply for an Order to Attend (N316) has on the second page a part where you can state particular questions you wish to put to the debtor and the documents you want them to bring to court.

If a debtor is served with the Order and does not turn up court, the County Court can pass the matter to a Circuit Judge to issue a suspended committal order, which will force him to attend court to purge his contempt and give the financial information. If he does not do so, a warrant for his arrest could be issued and the debtor may be sent to prison but this is a rare event.

SUMMARY

There are a number of methods available to enforce a County Court Judgment. You need to choose the appropriate method in the circumstances of the case. If you lack information about the Defendant's finances, an Order to Attend Court for Questioning might be worth considering.

APPENDIX A - COURT FORMS and EXTRACTS FROM COURT RULES

	In the County Court Money Claims Centre	
Claim Form	**Fee Account no.**	
		For court use only
	Claim no.	
	Issue date	

You may be able to issue your claim online which may save time and money.
Go to www.moneyclaim.gov.uk to find out more.

Claimant(s) name(s) and address(es) including postcode

Reeves Printing Ltd
10 Market Place
UPTON
UP10 2AB

SEAL

Defendant(s) name and address(es) including postcode

Mr Fred Smith
18 Victoria Street, UPTON, UP11 4TB

Brief details of claim

Debt Action
Unpaid invoice for the price of printing services

Value
£6,000 plus interest and cost

You must indicate your preferred County Court Hearing Centre for hearings here *(see notes for guidance)*

Upton County Court

Defendant's name and address for service including postcode	Mr Fred Smith 18 Victoria Street, UPTON, UP11 4T		£
		Amount claimed	6,050.00
		Court fee	455.00
		Legal representative's costs	
		Total amount	**£6,505.00**

For further details of the courts www.gov.uk/find-court-tribunal.
When corresponding with the Court, please address forms or letters to the Manager and always quote the claim number.

N1 Claim form (CPR Part 7) (05 14)   © Crown Copyright 2014

Claim No.	

Does, or will, your claim include any issues under the Human Rights Act 1998? ☐ Yes   ☑ No

Particulars of Claim (attached)(to follow)
1. The Claimant was acting in the course of business. The Defendant was acting as a professional writer.

2. The claim is for the agreed price of printing and book binding services.

3. The Claimant agreed to print and bid 1,000 copies of the Defendant's book on the terms and conditions signed on the 7 June xx/xx/xx, a copy of which are attached to these particulars of claim, for the agreed price of £6,000.

4. The contract included a term that the Claimant would not edit or proof read the manuscript received from the Defendant.

5. The Claimant received the manuscript from the Defendant, printed, and bound the books.

6. The terms of payment were 21 days from the date of delivery of the completed books. The Claimant delivered 1000 copies of the completed book on the xx/xx/xx and therefore payment for the Claimant's services became due on the xx/xx/xx.

7. The Claimant has not received payment and therefore claims the sum of £6,000 plus interest pursuant to section 69 of the County Courts Act 1984 at the rate of 8% per annum from the date payment became due to the date of this claim (xx/xx/xx) and continuing at a rate of £___

8. The Claimant has complied with Part III and IV of the Practice Direction on Pre-action Conduct and any relevant protocol.

AND THE CLAIMANT CLAIMS:

i. £6,000, plus

ii. interest being £50 and continuing at a daily rate of £_____

Statement of Truth
*(I believe)(The Claimant believes) that the facts stated in these particulars of claim are true.
* I am duly authorised by the claimant to sign this statement

Full name Michael John Langford Reeves

Name of claimant's legal representative's firm

signed   M J L Reeves

*(Claimant)(Litigation friend)
(Claimant's legal representative)

position or office held Director

(if signing on behalf of firm or company)

*delete as appropriate

Claimant's or claimant's legal representative's address to which documents or payments should be sent if different from overleaf including (if appropriate) details of DX, fax or e-mail.

Response Pack

You should read the 'notes for defendant' attached to the claim form which will tell you when and where to send the forms

Included in this pack are:

- either **Admission Form N9A**
  (if the claim is for a specified amount)
  or **Admission Form N9C**
  (if the claim is for an unspecified amount
  or is not a claim for money)

- either **Defence and Counterclaim Form N9B** (if the claim is for a specified amount)
  or **Defence and Counterclaim Form N9D**
  (if the claim is for an unspecified amount
  or is not a claim for money)

- **Acknowledgment of service**
  (see below)

Complete

If you admit the claim or the amount claimed and/or you want time to pay	the admission form
If you admit part of the claim	the admission form and the defence form
If you dispute the whole claim or wish to make a claim (a counterclaim) against the claimant	the defence form
If you need 28 days (rather than 14) from the date of service to prepare your defence, or wish to contest the court's jurisdiction	the acknowledgment of service
If you do nothing, judgment may be entered against you	

Acknowledgment of Service

Defendant's full name if different from the name given on the claim form

In the	Upton County Court
Claim No.	7UP00012
Claimant (including ref.)	Fred Bloggs
Defendant	Upton Energy Services Ltd

Address to which documents about this claim should be sent (including reference if appropriate)

Upton Energy Services Ltd
Upton House
River Road
Upton

	if applicable
fax no.	0111 999 666
DX no.	
Ref. no.	UES/123-01
e-mail	

Tel. no. 0111 333 444   Postcode UP1 1AX

Tick the appropriate box

1. I intend to defend all of this claim ✓
2. I intend to defend part of this claim ☐
3. I intend to contest jurisdiction ☐

(My) (Defendant's) date of birth is

If you file an acknowledgment of service but do not file a defence within 28 days of the date of service of the claim form, or particulars of claim if served separately, judgment may be entered against you.

If you do not file an application to dispute the jurisdiction of the court within 14 days of the date of filing this acknowledgment of service, it will be assumed that you accept the court's jurisdiction and judgment may be entered against you.

Signed	Position or office held	Managing Director	xx/xx/xx
(Defendant)(Defendant's solicitor)(Litigation friend)	(if signing on behalf of firm or company)		Date

The court office at

is open between 10 am and 4 pm Monday to Friday. When corresponding with the court, please address forms or letters to the Court Manager and quote the claim number.

N9 Response Pack (04.06)   HMCS

Defence and Counterclaim (specified amount)

- Fill in this form if you wish to dispute all or part of the claim and/or make a claim against the claimant (counterclaim).
- You have a limited number of days to complete and return this form to the court.
- Before completing this form, please read the notes for guidance attached to the claim form.
- Please ensure that all boxes at the top right of this form are completed. You can obtain the correct names and number from the claim form. The court cannot trace your case without this information.

How to fill in this form

- Complete sections 1 and 2. Tick the correct boxes and give the other details asked for.
- Set out your defence in section 3. If necessary continue on a separate piece of paper making sure that the claim number is clearly shown on it. In your defence you must state which allegations in the particulars of claim you deny and your reasons for doing so. **If you fail to deny an allegation it may be taken that you admit it.**
- If you dispute only some of the allegations you must
    - specify which you admit and which you deny; and
    - give your own version of events if different from the claimant's.

Name of court	Upton County Court
Claim No.	7UP00234
Claimant (including ref.)	REEVES PRINTING LTD
Defendant	FRED SMITH

- If you wish to make a claim against the claimant (a counterclaim) complete section 4.
- Complete and sign section 5 before sending this form to the court. Keep a copy of the claim form and this form.

Community Legal Service Fund (CLSF)

You may qualify for assistance from the CLSF (this used to be called 'legal aid') to meet some or all of your legal costs. Ask about the CLSF at any county court office or any information or help point which displays this logo.

1. How much of the claim do you dispute?

- [✓] I dispute the full amount claimed as shown on the claim form

    or
- [ ] I admit the amount of £ _____

    If you dispute only part of the claim you must **either**:
- pay the amount admitted to the person named at the address for payment on the claim form (see How to Pay in the notes on the back of, or attached to, the claim form). Then send this defence to the court

    or
- complete the admission form and this defence form and send them to the court.
    - [ ] I paid the amount admitted on (*date*) _____

        or
    - [ ] I enclose the completed form of admission (*go to section 2*)

2. Do you dispute this claim because you have already paid it? *Tick whichever applies*

- [ ] No (*go to section 3*)
- [ ] Yes   I paid £ _____ to the claimant

    on _____ (*before the claim form was issued*)

    Give details of where and how you paid it in the box below (*then go to section 3*)

    _____

3. Defence

I dispute the claim because the books which Reeves Printing delivered contained errors and were in a poor condition. I should not have to pay for books which were not of satisfactory quality because of a number of printing errors and the fact that the books were so badly bound that pages quickly fell out.

N9B Defence and Counterclaim (specified amount)(04.04)

HMCS

Directions questionnaire
(Small Claims Track)

In the	Claim No.
County Court Money Claims Centre	XX22BY203

To be completed by, or on behalf of,

Reeves Publishing Ltd

who is [1ˢᵗ][2ⁿᵈ][3ʳᵈ][   ][Claimant][Defendant][Part 20 claimant] in this claim

You should note the date by which this questionnaire must be returned and the name of the court it should be returned to since this may be different from the court where the proceedings were issued.

If you have settled this claim (or if you settle it on a future date) and do not need to have it heard or tried, you must let the court know immediately.

A Settlement/Mediation

Under the Civil Procedure Rules parties should make every effort to settle their case. At this stage you should still think about whether you and the other party(ies) can settle your dispute without going to a hearing.

You may seek to settle the claim either by direct discussion or negotiation with the other party or by mediation. If settlement is reached parties may enter into a binding agreement which can be enforced if the terms of the agreement were to be breached.

Mediation is a way of resolving disputes without a court hearing, where the parties are assisted in resolving their dispute with the help of an impartial mediator. If the claim is settled at this stage the parties can avoid further court fees, costs and time involved in preparing and attending a hearing.

You may use any mediation provider. However, HMCTS provide a **free confidential** Small Claims Mediation Service which is available to parties in most small claims cases which are for less than £10,000.

Mediation is usually carried out by telephone in one hour time limited appointments convenient to the parties and is quicker than waiting for a court hearing before a judge. There is no obligation to use the Small Claims Mediation Service nor are you required to settle if you do. If you are unable to reach agreement with the other party at mediation, the claim will proceed to a small claims hearing.

You can get more information about mediation from www.gov.uk

If all parties agree, this case will be referred to the Small Claims Mediation Service. In any event the court may order the service to contact you to explore mediation.

A1 Do you agree to this case being referred to the Small Claims Mediation Service?   ☑ Yes   ☐ No

Please give your contact details below – If all parties agree to mediation your details will be passed to the small claims mediation team who will contact you to arrange an appointment.

You must complete the remainder of the form regardless of your answer to A1

B Your contact details

Notes

Your full name

Reeves Publishing

Address for Service
10 Market Place
Upton
UP10 2AB

It's essential that you provide this information, particularly if you have requested mediation. Staff will contact you within office hours (9am – 5pm).

Telephone number	Mobile
0122 333 6666	

Email

reeves@fastbroadbank.co.uk

N180 Directions questionnaire (small claims track) (04.14)

C Track

C1 Do you agree that the small claims track is the appropriate track for this case? ☑ Yes ☐ No

If No, say why not and state the track to which you believe it should be allocated

Track
The small claims track — generally for lower value and less complex claims with a value under £10,000. You can get more information by reading leaflet EX306 'The small claims track in civil courts'. You can get this leaflet online from hmctsformfinder.justice.gov.uk

D About the hearing

Hearing venue

D1 At which County Court hearing centre would you prefer the small claims hearing to take place and why?
Upton County Court
This the local hearing centre for both parties

Location
If your claim is a designated money claim the case will usually be transferred to the claimant's preferred court or the defendant's home court, as appropriate. However, there is no guarantee of transfer to that court. For further information see CPR Parts 3, 12, 13, 14 and 26

Expert evidence

D2 Are you asking for the court's permission to use the written evidence of an expert? ☐ Yes ☑ No

If Yes, state why and give the name of the expert (if known) and the area of expertise and the likely cost if appointed.

Expert evidence
The court must grant you permission to use an expert witness. Your notice of allocation will tell you if permission has been granted. Please note the upper limit for expert's fees that can be recovered is £750. You can get more information by reading leaflet EX306 'The small claims track in civil courts'. You can get this leaflet online from hmctsformfinder.justice.gov.uk

Witnesses

D3 How many witnesses, including yourself, will give evidence on your behalf at the hearing? [1]

Witnesses
Witnesses may be asked to give evidence by either party. The court needs to have notice that you intend to call a witness. Witness expenses for travel accommodation and loss of earning should be met by the party requesting their attendance. You can get more information by reading EX342 'Coming to a court hearing'. You can get this leaflet online from hmctsformfinder.justice.gov.uk

Hearing

D4 Are there any days within the next six months when you, an expert or a witness will not be able to attend court for the hearing? ☑ Yes ☐ No

If Yes, please give details

	Dates **not** available
Yourself	1-8 August
Expert	
Other essential witness	

Will you be using an interpreter at the hearing either for yourself or for a witness? ☐ Yes ☑ No

If Yes, please specify the type of interpreter

Hearing
Dates to avoid: You should enter those dates where you, your expert or an essential witness will not be able to attend court because of a holiday or other commitments.

Interpreters: In some circumstances the court will arrange for, and meet the cost of an interpreter. If you require an interpreter, you should contact the court immediately. Further details visit our website www.justice.gov.uk under 'guidance'.

Notice of Allocation to the Small Claims Track	**In the UPTON COUNTY COURT**	
To Claimant	**Claim No.**	**7UP00333**
Carol Smith 22 River Crescent Upton UP2 4TH	**Claimant** (including ref.)	**Carol Smith**
	Defendant (including	**Clifford Jones**
	Date	**15 October**

District Judge Rutherford has considered the statements of case and allocation questionnaires filed and allocated the claim to **the small claims track.**

The hearing of this claim will take place at **Upton County Court 2pm on** _____

You must pay the court hearing fee of £_____ by _____ or the hearing will be removed from the court list.

The Judge has estimated that the hearing of this claim should take no longer than **90 minutes**. This is the total time for you, the other party and any witnesses to put your evidence and for the Judge to reach a decision. To help prepare the claim for hearing, the Judge has ordered that you comply with the following directions:—

1. Each party must deliver to every other party and to the court office copies of all documents on which he intends to rely at the hearing no later than 14 days before the hearing.

2.   Signed statements setting out the evidence of all witnesses on whom each party intends to rely must be prepared and copies included in the documents mentioned in paragraph 1. This includes the evidence of the parties themselves and of any other witness, whether or not he is going to come to court to give evidence.

Notes:
- If you cannot, or choose not to, attend the hearing, you must write and tell the court **at least 7 days before the date of the hearing**. The District Judge will hear the case in your absence, but will take account of your statement of case and any other documents you have filed.
- If you do not attend the hearing and do not give notice that you will not attend, the District Judge may strike out your claim, defence or counter claim. If the Claimant attends but the Defendant does not, the District Judge may make a decision based on the evidence of the Claimant only.
- Leaflets explaining more about what you should do and what happens when your case is allocated to the small claims track are available from the court office.

How to make successful small claims

 **Justice**

PART 27 - THE SMALL CLAIMS TRACK

Contents of this Part

Scope of this Part

27.1

(1) This Part –

(a) sets out the special procedure for dealing with claims which have been allocated to the small claims track under Part 26; and

(b) limits the amount of costs that can be recovered in respect of a claim which has been allocated to the small claims track.

(Rule 27.14 deals with costs on the small claims track)

(2) A claim being dealt with under this Part is called a small claim.

(Rule 26.6 provides for the scope of the small claims track. A claim for a remedy for harassment or unlawful eviction relating, in either case, to residential premises shall not be allocated to the small claims track whatever the financial value of the claim. Otherwise, the small claims track will be the normal track for –

- any claim which has a financial value of not more than £10,000 subject to the special provisions about claims for personal injuries and housing disrepair claims;
- any claim for personal injuries which has a financial value of not more than £10,000 where the claim for damages for personal injuries is not more than £1,000; and
- any claim which includes a claim by a tenant of residential premises against his landlord for repairs or other work to the premises where the estimated cost of the repairs or other work is not more than £1,000 and the financial value of any other claim for damages is not more than £1,000)

Back to top

Extent to which other Parts apply

27.2

(1) The following Parts of these Rules do not apply to small claims –

(a) Part 25 (interim remedies) except as it relates to interim injunctions$^{(GL)}$;

(b) Part 31 (disclosure and inspection);

(c) Part 32 (evidence) except rule 32.1 (power of court to control evidence);

(d) Part 33 (miscellaneous rules about evidence);

(e) Part 35 (experts and assessors) except rules 35.1 (duty to restrict expert evidence), 35.3 (experts – overriding duty to the court), 35.7 (court's power to direct that evidence is to be given by single joint expert) and 35.8 (instructions to a single joint expert);

(f) Subject to paragraph (3), Part 18 (further information);

(g) Part 36 (offers to settle); and

(h) Part 39 (hearings) except rule 39.2 (general rule– hearing to be in public).

(2) The other Parts of these Rules apply to small claims except to the extent that a rule limits such application.

(3) The court of its own initiative may order a party to provide further information if it considers it appropriate to do so.

Back to top

Court's power to grant a final remedy

27.3 The court may grant any final remedy in relation to a small claim which it could grant if the proceedings were on the fast track or the multi-track.

Back to top

Preparation for the hearing

27.4

(1) After allocation the court will –

(a) give standard directions and fix a date for the final hearing;

(b) give special directions and fix a date for the final hearing;

(c) give special directions and direct that the court will consider what further directions are to be given no later than 28 days after the date the special directions were given;

(d) fix a date for a preliminary hearing under rule 27.6; or

(e) give notice that it proposes to deal with the claim without a hearing under rule 27.10 and invite the parties to notify the court by a specified date if they agree the proposal.

(2) The court will –

(a) give the parties at least 21 days' notice of the date fixed for the final hearing, unless the parties agree to accept less notice; and

(b) inform them of the amount of time allowed for the final hearing.

(3) In this rule –

(a) 'standard directions' means –

(i) a direction that each party shall, at least 14 days before the date fixed for the final hearing, file and serve on every other party copies of all documents (including any expert's report) on which he intends to rely at the hearing; and

(ii) any other standard directions set out in Practice Direction 27; and

(b) 'special directions' means directions given in addition to or instead of the standard directions.

Back to top

Experts

27.5 No expert may give evidence, whether written or oral, at a hearing without the permission of the court.

(Rule 27.14(3)(d) provides for the payment of an expert's fees)

Back to top

Preliminary hearing

27.6

(1) The court may hold a preliminary hearing for the consideration of the claim, but only –

(a) where –

(i) it considers that special directions, as defined in rule 27.4, are needed to ensure a fair hearing; and

(ii) it appears necessary for a party to attend at court to ensure that he understands what he must do to comply with the special directions; or

(b) to enable it to dispose of the claim on the basis that one or other of the parties has no real prospect of success at a final hearing; or

(c) to enable it to strike out[GL] a statement of case or part of a statement of case on the basis that the statement of case, or the part to be struck out, discloses no reasonable grounds for bringing or defending the claim.

(2) When considering whether or not to hold a preliminary hearing, the court must have regard to the desirability of limiting the expense to the parties of attending court.

(3) Where the court decides to hold a preliminary hearing, it will give the parties at least 14 days' notice of the date of the hearing.

(4) The court may treat the preliminary hearing as the final hearing of the claim if all the parties agree.

(5) At or after the preliminary hearing the court will—

(a) fix the date of the final hearing (if it has not been fixed already) and give the parties at least 21 days' notice of the date fixed unless the parties agree to accept less notice;

(b) inform them of the amount of time allowed for the final hearing; and

(c) give any appropriate directions.

Back to top

Power of court to add to, vary or revoke directions

27.7 The court may add to, vary or revoke directions.

Back to top

Conduct of the hearing

27.8

(1) The court may adopt any method of proceeding at a hearing that it considers to be fair.

(2) Hearings will be informal.

(3) The strict rules of evidence do not apply.

(4) The court need not take evidence on oath.

(5) The court may limit cross-examination[GL].

(6) The court must give reasons for its decision.

Back to top

Non-attendance of parties at a final hearing

27.9

(1) If a party who does not attend a final hearing—

(a) has given written notice to the court and the other party at least 7 days before the hearing date that he will not attend;

(b) has served on the other party at least 7 days before the hearing date any other documents which he has filed with the court; and

(c) has, in his written notice, requested the court to decide the claim in his absence and has confirmed his compliance with paragraphs (a) and (b) above,

the court will take into account that party's statement of case and any other documents he has filed and served when it decides the claim.

(2) If a claimant does not –

(a) attend the hearing; and

(b) give the notice referred to in paragraph (1),

the court may strike out$^{(GL)}$ the claim.

(3) If –

(a) a defendant does not –

(i) attend the hearing; or

(ii) give the notice referred to in paragraph (1); and

(b) the claimant either –

(i) does attend the hearing; or

(ii) gives the notice referred to in paragraph (1),

the court may decide the claim on the basis of the evidence of the claimant alone.

(4) If neither party attends or gives the notice referred to in paragraph (1), the court may strike out the claim and any defence and counterclaim.

Back to top

Disposal without a hearing

27.10 The court may, if all parties agree, deal with the claim without a hearing.

Back to top

Setting judgment aside and re-hearing

27.11

(1) A party –

(a) who was neither present nor represented at the hearing of the claim; and

(b) who has not given written notice to the court under rule 27.9(1),

may apply for an order that a judgment under this Part shall be set aside$^{(GL)}$ and the claim re-heard.

(2) A party who applies for an order setting aside a judgment under this rule must make the application not more than 14

days after the day on which notice of the judgment was served on him.

(3) The court may grant an application under paragraph (2) only if the applicant –

(a) had a good reason for not attending or being represented at the hearing or giving written notice to the court under rule 27.9(1); and

(b) has a reasonable prospect of success at the hearing.

(4) If a judgment is set aside –

(a) the court must fix a new hearing for the claim; and

(b) the hearing may take place immediately after the hearing of the application to set the judgment aside and may be dealt with by the judge who set aside the judgment.

(5) A party may not apply to set aside a judgment under this rule if the court dealt with the claim without a hearing under rule 27.10.

Rules 27.12 and 27.13 are revoked.

Back to top

Costs on the small claims track

27.14

(1) This rule applies to any case which has been allocated to the small claims track ~~unless paragraph (5) applies~~.

(Rules 46.11 and 46.13 make provision in relation to orders for costs made before a claim has been allocated to the small claims track)

(2) The court may not order a party to pay a sum to another party in respect of that other party's costs, fees and expenses, including those relating to an appeal, except –

(a) the fixed costs attributable to issuing the claim which –

(i) are payable under Part 45; or

(ii) would be payable under Part 45 if that Part applied to the claim;

(b) in proceedings which included a claim for an injunction or an order for specific performance a sum not exceeding the amount specified in Practice Direction 27 for legal advice and assistance relating to that claim;

(c) any court fees paid by that other party;

(d) expenses which a party or witness has reasonably incurred in travelling to and from a hearing or in staying away from home for the purposes of attending a hearing;

(e) a sum not exceeding the amount specified in Practice Direction 27 for any loss of earnings or loss of leave by a party or witness due to attending a hearing or to staying away from home for the purposes of attending a hearing;

(f) a sum not exceeding the amount specified in Practice Direction 27 for an expert's fees;

(g) such further costs as the court may assess by the summary procedure and order to be paid by a party who has behaved unreasonably; ~~and~~

(h) the Stage 1 and, where relevant, the Stage 2 fixed costs in rule 45.18 where –

(i) the claim was within the scope of the Pre-Action Protocol for Low Value Personal Injury Claims in Road Traffic Accidents ('the RTA Protocol') or the Pre-action Protocol for Low Value Personal Injury (Employers' Liability and Public Liability) Claims ('the EL/PL Protocol'):

(ii) the claimant reasonably believed that the claim was valued at more than the small claims track limit in accordance with paragraph 4.1(4) of the relevant Protocol; and

(iii) the defendant admitted liability under the process set out in the relevant Protocol; but

(iv) the defendant did not pay those Stage 1 and, where relevant, Stage 2 fixed costs; and

(i) in an appeal, the cost of any approved transcript reasonably incurred.

(3) A party's rejection of an offer in settlement will not of itself constitute unreasonable behaviour under paragraph (2)(g) but the court may take it into consideration when it is applying the unreasonableness test.

(4) The limits on costs imposed by this rule also apply to any fee or reward for acting on behalf of a party to the proceedings charged by a person exercising a right of audience by virtue of an order under section 11 of the Courts and Legal Services Act 1990[1] (a lay representative).

~~5 Where – a the financial value of a claim exceeds the limit for the small claims track; but b the claim has been allocated to the small claims track in accordance with rule 26.7(3), the small claims track costs provisions will apply unless the parties agree that the fast track costs provisions are to apply.~~

~~6 Where the parties agree that the fast track costs provisions are to apply, the claim and any appeal will be treated for the purposes of costs as if it were proceeding on the fast track except that trial costs will be in the discretion of the court and will not exceed the amount set out for the value of claim in rule 46.2 (amount of fast track trial costs).~~

Back to top

Claim re-allocated from the small claims track to another track

27.15 Where a claim is allocated to the small claims track and subsequently re-allocated to another track, rule 27.14 (costs on the small claims track) will cease to apply after the claim has been re-allocated and the fast track or multi-track costs rules will apply from the date of re-allocation.

Back to top

Footnotes

1.   1990 c.41. Back to text

COURT FEES   *(correct as of May 2014)*

Online services

HM Courts & Tribunals Service has two internet based services: Money Claim Online (MCOL) for some money claims up to the value of £99,999.99, and Possession Claim Online (PCOL) for possessions concerning rent or mortgage arrears. You can use either of these simple, convenient and secure processes and pay a reduced fee.

For more information ask court staff or visit our websites:

www.moneyclaim.gov.uk
www.possessionclaim.gov.uk

Civil court fees

Starting your claim

Money claims

To issue a claim for money, the following fees will be payable based on the amount claimed, including interest:

	Court issued claim	Money Claim Online (MCOL)
up to £300	£35	£25
£300.01 – £500	£50	£35
£500.01 – £1,000	£70	£60
£1,000.01 – £1,500	£80	£70
£1,500.01 – £3,000	£115	£105
£3,000.01 – £5,000	£205	£185
£5,000.01 – £15,000	£455	£410
£15,000.01 – £50,000	£610	£550
£50,000.01 – £100,000	£910	£815*
£100,000.01 – £150,000	£1,115	N/A
£150,000.01 – £200,000	£1,315	N/A
£200,000.01 – £250,000	£1,515	N/A
£250,000.01 – £300,000	£1,720	N/A
more than £300,000 or an unlimited amount	£1,920	N/A

*Maximum amount for money claims on MCOL is £99,999.99

Hearing fees

Small Claim Track where the amount claimed is:

up to £300	£25
between £300.01 and £500	£55
between £500.01 and £1,000	£80
between £1,000.01 and £1,500	£115
between £1,500.01 and £3,000	£170
more than £3,000	£335

APPENDIX B

USEFUL CONTACTS AND SOURCES OF INFORMATION

Websites:

1. www.justice.gov.uk

The Ministry of Justice website contains the latest civil court rules and court forms, as well as the latest level of court fees.

2. www.firstreport.co.uk

First Report provides credit reports on Limited Companies, Non-Limited Businesses and Company Directors. The information is useful when deciding if a Defendant has the funds to make it worth pursuing a claim.

3. www.hceoa.org.uk

This is website for the High Court Enforcement Officers Association. This site will be a good starting point if you need to consider which High Court Enforcement company you might want to instruct if you have a Judgment debt to enforce.

4. www.bailii.org

This website provides free access to law reports

5. www.small-claims-mediation.co.uk

Small Claims Mediation Ltd is a company that provides online and telephone mediation.

6. www.trustonline.org.uk

Trust Online is the online service of Registry Trust Ltd which keeps the register of County Court Judgment. This site will enable you to check online for County Court Judgments that are recorded against individuals and businesses.

7. www.citizensadvice.org.uk

This website from the Citizens Advice Bureau will not provide you will details of how to contact your local advice centre.

8. www.moneyclaim.gov.uk

Money Claim Online is a way of making or responding to a money claim on the internet.

Addresses

9. County Court Money Claims Centre:

P.O.Box 527
Salford
Greater Manchester
M5 0BY

Lightning Source UK Ltd.
Milton Keynes UK
UKOW06f0414111117
312492UK00014B/862/P